The Fool's

Journey

Raise the Vibe - Heal

the Tribe

By Bradley Philpott

Acknowledgements

In every book, there is blood, sweat and tears. In my life, there have been people and moments that changed me forever and helped me carve my path. There are so many that stood as bricks to build my solid foundation that I could write a book about those people alone. Maybe I will someday.

Maya Angelou once said, When I go on stage to speak, I bring everyone that has ever been kind to me. I love her imagery! When I step into my studio to help my clients, I bring everyone who has ever been kind to me. Each one of you lend your Light and Love to the work I do.

Thank you for being my host of angels on
Earth.

To my Mom and my Dad - Thank you for
giving me life. Thank you for giving me the
best life you possibly could. Your undying
work and dedication has let me chase every
dream I could conceive and has provided a
soft place to land when the world gets
harsh. I love you

To my friends - Traci M., Hillary S., Emily S.,
Courtney F., Jeff D., Courtney M., Steven
G., Marcus L., Jeanne Cauthron, Wes S.,
Nora S., Jo S, Mathue S., Anthony B., Tyler
H., and so many more. Without you, I have
no idea where I would've ended up. Many of
you shaped my life and helped guide me
when I was disconnected from my path. You

saw potential and beauty in my life, in my work when I saw darkness. I thank you for being Light Beacons for me! Your reflection is the greatest gift to me. I'm am ever grateful for your kindness, compassion, love and grace.

To my many teachers and guides, Kim Hayes, thank you for giving me a voice. To Timido Ricard, thank you for walking beside me during my initiation. To Julie Webb, thank you for believing in me and giving me a space to start my work! To Teri Alsip, thank you for being my soul sister and constant voice of reason. To Angie Ditto, thank you for showing me how to see in the dark. Heather Brownstone, thank you for teaching me you can be both honest and kind. Tracey Oden, thank you for taking me in and helping me heal when I had nowhere to go. To Dan and Jeanne Cauthron, thank you for believing in me for being my Earth Queen and Web guru! To Amber Dowell & Taylar Townzen & G. Desiree Fultz, thank you for believing in me and giving me wings to fly! And finally, to Nan McClain, thank you for telling me to be assertive, to share my insights because it can save lives and to believe in myself!

Thank you to my clients, my family and my friends. You all touch my heart. I'm wrapped in your love and support. I will wear my armor proudly!

To you, reader of these pages, be gentle with yourself. Don't be afraid, it's not scary! You'll make it! Above all else, love yourself.

INTRODUCTION

Welcome to the New Earth!

If you have chosen this book, then you are well on your way to ascending to your Highest Self! Many point to December 21, 2012 as the End of The World. In a way, it was. We were all given a clean slate to travel the multiverse in new and dynamic ways.

The Mayans were amazing seers and ended their calendar on December 21, 2012. The date ended the cycle of Pisces energy, also known as the Age of Pisces. We are now moving through the Dawn of the Age of Aquarius. The new era, or epoch, is different in many ways to the ages that have come before. It's the New Earth!

The New Earth is vibrationally different than ages past. Ages like Aries, Pisces and Capricorn for example are completely different elementally and fundamentally than Aquarius.

During the age of Aries, in forgotten times, people sacrificed the Ram as a sacred gift to Creator. They used the scapegoat to gather their sins and cast them out of the community.

During the age of Pisces, a man named Yeshua walked on water. He healed the sick and the poor. He surged against the current of his era, like a salmon swimming upstream. He called others to follow him. He created a bountiful feast out of a small sack of bread and fish. The symbol for his growing followers was the ichthus, a picture of a fish.

As we move into the Age of Aquarius, the energy has shifted once again. The old ways are passed. Karma that was created is now erased. The slate has been wiped clean. You can march to the beat of your own drum. You don't have to practice ritual and ceremony by rote, you can follow your

 intuition and your own inner voice to create new and profound ways of being!

Aquarians are rebels, Aquarians are rule breakers, they are always moving, they truly embody the gypsy life. Yet they are nurturing, they give you space and they march forward breaking through seeming obstacles with ease.

Aquarian energy is the fresh second wind. You can do things now that you were unable to do before. Every step you take is the right one. Trust each step.

Aquarian energy asks each of us to stand sovereign in our own power. Be sure of yourself. Enjoy and celebrate the journey! Move and shake like never before. You were born, here in this time to make a difference. If you have a pulse, then you have a purpose.

Finding that purpose may be easier or harder than you think. When we're children, we get asked again and again, "What do you want to be when you grow up?"

Our child brain gives so many different answers. It's like our future is carried on the whim of the wind. One day we want to be an astronaut, the next we want to be a veterinarian. That is how the young brain works. With each new stimulus, we change and alter our perception of the world and of ourselves.

You are no longer a child. You have chosen a path and you are paving the way forward. It has been hard work. You have reaped rewards. You have even made mistakes. Thank goodness for mistakes, they teach us lessons and help us grow. You have grown so much and you probably don't even realize it.

You are in the process of becoming. Like the fool, you are open, ambitious, full of ideas and excitement!

In the pages ahead, you will discover ways to tap into your subconscious mind and begin to direct your journey in pursuit of your life path.

Enjoy the ride! Take in the views! Above all else, love yourself through this.

Seeker - This book is for you!
You have found the road. Now, let's walk
the path   together.

"The journey of 1000 miles begins with a single step."

-Ancient Chinese Proverb

My path is the path of the Fool. Learn from my follies, laugh with me at my blunders but most of all rejoice that we are alive and experiencing history in the making. The dawning of a new age. The birth of an epoch. Poets will write of this time of wonderment, song will be sung about our adventures and tragedies. Life is the grandest epic ever written. Be bold! Be free! Be YOU!

Chapter Zero
The Fool

The Fool awakens from his sleep,

His slumber long and rest deep.

Spirit is calling on the wind and rain,

A tourniquet of healing from sorrow from

pain.

Pushed to the edge He walks without care,

Wherever He steps guiding Spirit is there.

Turn towards the Light and fret not,

The Journey before you is the greatest story

ever wrought.

Element: Spirit

Blessing: New Beginnings

Challenge: Letting Go

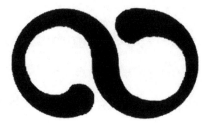

Life begins as a journey of self discovery.
Spirit has led you here in subtle ways.
Nudging you to take your life into your own
hands. Asking you to free your mind, open
your heart and awaken your soul.

We all begin the path to enlightenment as the Fool. Like a newborn babe, we are scared, cold and in shock with the bitter harshness of reality. Our eyes search every space for a familiar face but we are greeted by strangers and shadows in every corner. Some of the faces are kind and gentle. Others are sweet fruit with rotted worms at the core. Still yet there are others with malice but deep down hearts of gold. And others are quiet spectators that sit and listen.

My journey of self discovery began over 12 years ago, I was living with my partner of ten years at the time. I had adopted the idea of the American Dream. I was in debt up to my eyeballs. I was working two jobs to pay off credit cards and student loans. I had a bonus daughter that filled my life with joy but I warred often with her mother. My partner wasn't awake or supportive and wanted me to hide my light. He meant well. A bright flame draws too many night creatures. I could almost sense his fear that I would be hurt if I shined too brightly.

You see - the world doesn't want you to shine. People in your lives don't want you to succeed. They don't want you to move out of their comfort zones. They can't help it. Deep down they want you to be happy. But many people still operate in the realm of fear.

In life there are really only 2 emotions:
    1) Fear

2) Love

All other emotions can be traced back to these two foundational elements. We live in a universe of duality. Good vs. Evil. Light vs. Dark. Male vs. Female. Young vs. Old.

Creator made this reality so that we might experience a full spectrum of emotions. You see without duality, free will cannot exist. There has to be a choice. Do you choose good or do you choose evil? That is the driving force behind the very fabric of three dimensional reality. Cause and Effect.

But what if I told you that you don't have to stay in three dimensional reality? What if there was something beyond that? Stephen Hawking- a theoretical physicist and one of the greatest minds of our modern time believed in a theory called the multiverse. A multiverse is many universes occupying the same space. Think of it as a stack of papers, each paper is a universe. But instead of becoming thicker with each layer, the stack remains the same size there is just more there.

The multiverse we inhabit is filled with all manner of beasts. Humans. Angels. Gods and Goddesses. Mythical Creatures and more!

At the beginning of my journey I knew nothing about different dimensions, multiverse theory, ascension, cosmic consciousness or channeling. You could say I was asleep. Not a deep sleep, but a fretful one near the end of my rest cycle. My limbs were waking and I knew there had to be something more. The Bible talked about it. The Quran mentioned it numerous times. I saw dignified initiates in shows and read their wisdom in books but it fell on a stone heart and dead ears. I snored through the alarm clock the multiverse was trying to use to gently wake my sleeping mind.

You see - I had a calling. A calling from God to be a Witness, to be a minister. Which manifested as a need to fix everyone. I took on everyone's burdens. My partners imbalance, my daughter's fears, my partners ex-wife's guilt, my parent's worry, my boss's frustrations and every friend I met had another burden to place on my shoulders. I just kept piling them on like a pack animal. Oh you have marriage problems?! Here let me lighten your load! You're struggling from depression?! Let me ease your mind. On and on I labored.

One day while working in a portrait studio, I experienced a premonition. I saw myself quenched in fire and poured into a crucible. The crucible shined with golden light and I was placed into a mold. I know now this was a prophetic vision of what was to come.

That very day, my back exploded like lightning. Electricity raced up my spine and exploded in a fireworks display of colors in my head. I crumpled to the ground. I couldn't move. I could distantly hear my coworker's frets and ministrations. But the world fell away and I was consumed by pain and Light.

My journey had begun. You see that is what awakening looks like. A pain more painful than any you've ever experienced. A vision of a future you can't understand. And a feeling that you're all alone. You are nothing. You are dust. And yet you are never alone. You are connected to all things. And you are stardust! Then as quickly as it had come the feeling vanished.

I suffered what is called a Spontaneous Awakening. Awakening usually happens after years of study. Hours upon hours of diligent meditation. Pouring over sacred texts and filling your mind with grander ideas and thoughts. After courting the universe year after year, suddenly the light bulb comes on, the universe shows up and your mind is blown by the experience. Mine happened in a Wal-Mart portrait studio. Not exactly a temple or monastery.

I had done all these things. I'm a recovering Southern Baptist. My studies of the Bible began almost before I could talk. I guess you could say I was born to be devout. My mother attended church while she carried me in her womb. Her shirt would bounce to the music as I kept the beat. I still can't resist tapping my foot to a good rhythm.

For years, I studied the Bible. Pondered scripture. Divined the purpose and meaning behind words written thousands of years ago. The Bible is believed to be the living word of God. I believe that is well and good. For some.

Have you heard of the movie, "God's Not Dead!" A huge phenomenon within the Christian community. A sequel was even recorded at my alma mater, John Brown University. The message is that God is not dead. He is alive. His word is living and breathing. He speaks to us daily through his word.

Now, here is where things get tricky.

 Many Christians will tell you that to edit or add to scripture is sacrilegious. However, everyone knows about the Council of Nicea.The First Council of Nicaea was a council of Christian bishops convened in the

Bithynian city of Nicaea by the Roman Emperor Constantine I in AD 325. Many churches quote it's creed to this very day.

Let me break it down for you. The council was created to take all these convoluted, conflicting, bizarre and controversial scriptures, letters and teachings and make them fit into a neat little book. Basically, editing the word of God. The exact thing they preached against. They did. The book they voted on and edited is what we call the Bible in our modern world.

What if I told you that Spirit, God, Goddess, Odin, Zeus, Brahma, Krishna - whatever you call Creator Spirit still talks today? Not from a book that some bishops cut and pasted together from some forgotten pottery but Spirit actually says, "Hi (insert your name) may I sit and talk for awhile?"

[Throughout this book I will use many names to describe Creator Spirit, Godself or The I AM. Please use whatever language suits your walk best. This is your journey after all. Don't get hung up on the vocabulary. There's bigger fish to fry here.]

If you have felt the calling you know what I say to be true. Spirit is calling you. Do you stay in bed, nice and cozy protected from the outside world? Or do you take a leap of faith and believe that wherever the Universe is calling you will be a place that is for your highest good and to help you find your life's purpose?

You are an integral part of the fabric of reality. The Universe will always support you in your walk. The Fool knows that. He trusts in all things. Like a babe trusting his parents, we must trust that Spirit knows the world better than we do. For some of us, trusting the universe is hard. Not every parent had the best intentions when raising their children.

If that is you, stop right now.

Let go of that fear.

Spirit is not like your parents here on Earth. Do not make the mistake of distrusting Spirit. The Universe needs you to play your part seamlessly so the whole can maintain integrity. Some would argue, 'As above, So

Below.' "Well Bradley, my parents were awful so Spirit must be too." While that is in fact true. Relatively speaking, a copy is never an exact copy. As the layers are peeled back from the dimension that Spirit resides in to the third dimension that our corporeal bodies reside in, the image gets fuzzier and more distorted as you go. Imagine making a copy of a copy about 1000 times. You ever do that on a printer? After about twenty five, the image gets softer and less focused until you can barely tell what the original was supposed to be. That pretty much explains our problem.

We were made to be perfect beings but as our spirit was distilled, compressed and squished into a flesh sack, we lost some of our original integrity. We are poor copies of the original blueprint. Either from breeding or whether it is the process of transitioning from higher dimensions to the 3rd dimension, we lose a lot of our true selves.

So how do we get back to source? How do we get back to the original copy?

Feel the vibes!

Vibration is the key. The Fool's Journey is about seeking the right frequency to tap into the original vibration of source. Tune your antenna to pick up the proper signal. Luckily, ancient teachings have been passed down from generation to generation to aid us in this process.

I will use all of my training, education and experience to help you along your journey. Over the course of my life, I have had the opportunity to study Greek mythology, Norse mythology, Christianity, Judaism, Shamanism, Soul Alchemy, Human Design, Eastern medicine and energy healing, reflexology, oils and herbs, numerology and so much more. I will utilize every lesson I have learned to help you raise your vibration so you can learn to fly on the wings of the eagle's and commune with Spirit.

The 'logos' or 'word', in English, is alive and well. The veil is rent and has not been closed. God's not dead. Spirit is truly alive. Spirit is talking to you daily. Communing with your heart, if only you would look up,

listen inward and raise your vibration to
match Source, the OG Frequency of Love!

Aum - the origin of the big bang

The first word of creation

CHAPTER 1

The Magician

Power plays upon His hands,

Wind, Rain, Fire and Land!

If he can dream it,

The world is at His command.

Powers of insight, ruler of his domain.

Learn the secrets,

Never be the same.

Element: Earth

Zodiac: Capricorn

Blessings: Magic

Challenge: Balance

Living a magical life is not fairy dust, unicorns and dragon slaying. Don't get me wrong - you'll slay dragons. But not all dragons have scales. Your Angel's may not appear to you in bright shining clouds of glory and a heavenly chorus. I'm not saying they can't. However, it takes a lot of energy to manifest a whole heavenly host on our plane so I wouldn't get your hopes up.

Instead, angels, spirits and other beings communicate on our realm in different ways. In Chapter 1, we will talk about psychic ability. Whether you 'see' Spirit is defined by your psychic ability. You can also hear it, see clues through signs like 11:11, divination, or other physical means. For the most part, you will find patterns and synchronicities are used often with spirits and angels.

It's all about noticing the grand design unfolding. If we believe that all life is connected through energy and frequency, then won't there be ripples in our direction when something is about to happen? For example, Scientists predict the weather by examining patterns and record keeping to predict what will happen next. They only get it right about 75% of the time. It's a common joke in my hometown, that if we were as terrible at our job as Weathercasters, then we'd be fired! It's funny but at the same time it illustrates a HUGE point I'm about to make.

You're psychic! Yes - You! You obviously know that if you picked up this book in the esoteric or occult section of your book store. Thank goodness for Barnes & Noble - doesn't it smell amazing in there?

Anyway, you are not going to be right 100% of the time. Gasp! I know. Don't panic. Even the best athletes only have about a 50% average during the season. Yes, I just made a sports reference. If you know me, be amazed and astounded. I know some sports. Don't get crazy. I still can't keep score.

There are some amazing, gifted, and talented psychics out there who have bad days. They may not say your Father's name perfectly. But I want you to understand, they may actually be talking to your Father, it is also up to the Spirit and the energy around each other that helps messages come in clearly. Sometimes, Mercury will be in retrograde. And all hell breaks loose!

So give these people and your blossoming gifts a break! People make mistakes. Psychics have bad days. You will get something wrong. I assure you. Don't get hung up on it! Keep going. It's okay to fail, at least you showed up and gave Spirit a listening ear.

My favorite story is about my client Nan McClain. You see I began seeing her early in my practice, for a while she couldn't visit because her Parkinson's disease didn't allow her to brave the stairs. I was working in a salon at the time with an upstairs studio. Nan's first visit happened downstairs in a salon chair among hair dryers and curling irons because the salon was downstairs and stairs were a point of trepidation for her. Nan never forgot her first experience. I remember her being surprised that Reiki could affect her the way it did.

Cut to a few months later, I am travelling to her house once a week because her disease has made her house bound. I performed Light Reiki and Reflexology on her each session. For 6 weeks, I told her that something was wrong on the Right side of her head and neck. She shrugged off my concerns certain that it was merely scar tissue.

A few months before she had had a procedure done where electrodes were attached to her brain to stimulate regions that dealt with her tremors. The battery pack was placed in her right chest and the wires ran from there, up her neck to her brain. She said what I was picking up was the pack.

Finally, after 6 weeks of listening to my steady, gentle advice, Nan called her Neurologist. He got her in immediately. That worried her.

For another 6 weeks I didn't hear from her. Unbeknownst to me, Nan was having emergency surgeries to remove the wires and battery pack because 4 different types of infection had settled in her apparatus. We were both right! It was her battery and wires. And something was definitely wrong!

My hands and intuition picked up on something she couldn't. Her body wasn't signaling anything wrong. She felt healthy as ever. But she was slowly succumbing to a vicious infection. It was silently killing her.

Shortly after she got done with her surgeries and rehab, Nan bumped into me in the grocery store. She walked up to me and said, "I don't know whether to kiss you or slap you!" She continued to tell me about her battle with the infections, her stint at the hospital and the painful recovery.

"You knew all along. You saved my life, Bradley!" She looked at me with tears streaming down her face. "Why didn't you make me call sooner. I could've died!"

I told her I didn't trust myself. I was still learning how everything worked and I took her opinion over my intuition. I failed her.

"You didn't fail me." Nan put her hands on my shoulders. "You failed yourself. Now, don't you ever mistrust yourself again. Believe in yourself. Your power saved my life!"

And Spirit did. My gifts are here to help heal people. Help them see where rot and infection is in their body, mind and spirit. Not every disease or problem is physical. I can see them all. Never mistrust yourself. As you walk this journey, listen to your inner wisdom, that inner voice will not let you down.

Learn to see as I see.

Trust in your power!

Now, let's press on shall we? We've come to grips with the fact that we're not going to be 100% accurate. How do ensure that you are 100% and ready to go?

"When you recognize that there is a voice inside your head that pretends to be you and never stops speaking, you are awakening out of your unconscious identification with the stream of thinking. When you notice that voice, you realize that who you are is not that voice- the thinker - but the one who is aware of it."

~Eckhart Tolle

Lesson 1

Creating Sacred Space

Go within, Find your center. Find that quiet place.

We have all heard these yogic mantras before. The Thinker. The Heart. The Holy Spirit. The Soul. The Silent Witness. It goes by many names because it has been discovered and rediscovered.

As a race, humanity is very forgetful. History is written by the conquerors and the ones in power. Stories don't always survive from generation to generation. Sometimes the narrative doesn't fit the times, sometimes it is slaughtered as clans and tribes are killed off or die out.

I call this inner wisdom and thinker, The Silent Witness. Each new iteration of the Silent Witness brings each subsequent generation to a collective consciousness. The Akashic Records, the Book of Life, the Kabbalistic Secrets all dwell here. There is a rhyme and reason deep in this quiet place. The chaos of the outside world fades away and you are able to perceive infinity, the perfect tessellation of the universe.
How do you get down to this Silent Witness?

Taking that step is the beginning of Shamanic work and Journey. For me, it begins as I create sacred space. Sacred Space is essential for your protection, healing and self awareness. Creating sacred space readies our mind, body and soul to commune with Spirit, within and without of ourselves.

Think of sacred space as a microcosm of the universe. We create a sphere of influence that we work ritual, ceremony and journey in. What is done in the circle is sent out at the end of each work. Remember, As Above, So Below. What happens in the circle effects the outside world. It ripples through the fabric of the universe seeking out your intent for your highest good.

The reason each of us has the sovereignty to do this is found within our birthright. We are Spiritual Beings having a Human Experience! Wrap your head around that for second…

You are a Spiritual Being!

Just by being you, your birthright gives you power and dominion over your reality. Learning this was a hard pill for me to swallow.

Wait? So you're saying I chose this broken relationship?
My Aunt chose to be broken in body and mind at the age of 16?
I wanted to be in that car wreck?
I wanted to see someone die before my eyes? Witness their last breath?

Yes. You chose each and every experience. With your thoughts, you send out the desire of your heart. Your heart creates energy that is sent out on the waves of thought, constantly drawing experiences that match your frequency.

The esoteric community calls this The Law of Attraction. Like calls to like. Quite simple really.

When you own your thoughts and guard them, you begin taking measures to adjust or even transform your reality to create the perfect place for your soul to exist. Sacred Space will help you do this with focus and intent. But the mystery is to walk in this way at all times. Be sovereign at all times. Manifest the right thoughts for your soul purpose.

Creating Sacred Space:

You do not need any tools, or instruments to create sacred space. The power is in your intent and will. Think it. Believe it. And so shall it be.

Stand facing the East.
Raise your hands in invocation.
As I speak, I lower my hands and visualize a golden curtain being pulled down. The barrier or shield is gossamer and opaque but strong as spider silk.

Hail! Powers of the East!
Sanctuary of Fire and the Soul!
Bless and consecrate this space.
May passion spur my will to fight.

Walk or turn to the South.

Hail! Powers of the South!

Halls of Air and the Mind!

Bless and consecrate this space.

May my thoughts be clear and concise.

Walk or turn to the West

Hail! Powers of the West!

Fountain of Water and the Heart!

Bless and consecrate this space.

May my intent ripple outward for the highest good.

Walk or turn to the North.

Hail! Powers of the North!
Temple of Earth and the Body!
Bless and consecrate this space.
May my body be able and willing.

Turn towards the center of the circle.
Raise your hands and then lower them as
you say,

As Above, So Below.

Put your arms straight out and then move
towards your heart. Placing them in prayer
position.

As without, so within.
Father & Mother,
I thank you for this moment.

I come in gratitude for all the work you do on my behalf.

Seen and unseen.

I thank you for my breath. My pulse. My thoughts.

They are the tools of creation.

Left behind long ago for us to find.

Thank you for guiding me through this life.

Guard and protect this space as I work.

As my guardians and guides join hands with me.

We praise you!

In Yeshua's name we pray, Amen!

(Note: Choose any deity you like for this exercise. It should feel real to you. Connect within your soul. The more of a connection the stronger the work. Play around with it. We'll talk more about this in subsequent chapters.)

For now that is a great way to protect your room, your home and your place of work. We will discuss other ways of creating this space and altering it for your specific needs. But for now, practice raising this circle and get it down to where it is second nature.

Warning - you will stumble through words. You will blank out. You will skip parts or go in the wrong direction even. That's okay. Go with it. Laugh at yourself as Spirit smiles down and know that it is perfect for this moment, for your path. Not everyone is hooked on pomp and circumstance. It's okay to wing it. The most important thing is your intent and your will behind the creation. That is the key!

Practice!

Practice!

Practice!

I'm serious. Do this until you can do it in your sleep, backwards and forwards. It will take dedication. It will take time. How do you think musicians learn and grow? Practice!

You will never know what you are capable of until you just do it! For some, we need permission to act. For others, you just do it. Either way, I'm telling you to go practice. This is your invitation to unleash your inner wisdom!

How do you feel now?

I feel at home in sacred space. It feels like a warm hug. Like being wrapped up in warm blankets on a crisp October morning. Sigh. Perfection!

What do you notice about the room when you perform this exercise?

For me, the air always gets thicker and sound carries a ping or a sharp echo. The air feels a little more dense or palpable. And there's a tiny pressure fluctuation that is detected by my inner ear.

If you perform a ceremony, a ritual or if you raise energy. You want to release the circle. For journeys or dream work and sometimes healing work, I leave the circle as it is. Its power will dissipate naturally and flow where it needs to go. Releasing the circle gives it a little boost. It's like throwing a rock in a pond. Whoosh! It ripples out into eternity.

To release the Circle:

Raise your hands up and push them down like you're parting the Red Sea.

The circle is dispelled but never broken.

I visualize it rippling outward in an ever widening ring seeking my goals and dreams. The energy will find similar frequencies and bring them back.

A note on visualization and spellwork:

Some ripples return sooner than others.Think of visualization and spell work like ordering something from Amazon. Some shipments come all at once or in smaller packages so you can get little gifts in a timely manner. Don't judge the efficacy of your work on whether it brought you exactly what you needed, instead focus on the gifts, tools and lessons it brings to place you in the most ideal spot to manifest your will. You can move any mountain one shovel at a time. It's usually not that arduous, but it can be.

Let's say you wished for a brand new sports car.

Just because a new Porsche doesn't show up with big red bow doesn't mean your ritual didn't work. The universe may offer you a promotion. That's ripple one returning. Then it helps you get a 401K that has a policy where you can borrow against yourself. That's step 2. An email arrives in your Inbox that is from the Sports Car dealership. That's step 3. You walk into the dealership and your cousin or friend or Uncle is the car salesman. That's step 4. They cut you a major deal. Your payments are perfect. That's step 5. You now hold the keys to that Porsche you've always dreamed of! It's yours. No it didnt show up on your doorstep. You still had to do the leg work to help it manifest but the universe guided you all the way!

In 5 easy steps, it manifested your goal for you. Sometimes, the steps take more time to return. It doesn't mean your spell is ineffective it means that something in your journey or your thoughts is blocking it.

You're being met with resistance. Or it's not for your highest good.

I can wish to be the Queen of England but that is more than likely not going to happen. Unless of course, I perform shady or immoral acts which the universe very well could lead me to, I would use common sense to understand that the price of failure would be intolerable at best and deadly at the worst. Use discernment in all things. There is a Darkness and Light inherent in the Universe. Without one, the other does not exist. So it must be to keep the universe in balance. Choose the steps that feel right. The ones that sing to your soul. Make your heart pitter patter and leap. That's the right choice.

The Hopi have a saying, "The longest journey you'll ever take, is the walk from the heart to the head."

Lesson 2

The Dream Journal

When you first begin to experience psychic and paranormal phenomena, you may not always get clear and concise information.

Either you're not tuning into the right frequency or Spirit is trying to talk to you in a way you have not perceived yet. Sometimes the signal will come in spotty. I joked about Mercury Retrograde, but seriously watch out.

Mercury is the planet of communication, obviously talking to the dead fall within his domain. Mercury, or Hermes as the Greeks called him, flew back and forth from the realm of the gods on Mt. Olympus to the mortal realm to carry out orders and messages between the living and the divine. At some point, he got tired so he hired Shamans. And that is how the first Shaman was born.

That is not canon. You won't find that in Aristotle or Plato's works. Although fascinating, I like the idea. We no longer walk among gods and monsters. We walk among mortals and we're set apart. We're gifted.

The divine speaks to everyone. But I look at it like this. Everyone can sing. Not everyone can sing well. So you have to find your niche. Over the next few chapters, we'll explore various ways to communicate with Spirit and to fine tune the dial so you can tap into a clear message.

One great way to start is a dream journal. Spirit can't always get our attention when we're out there living life. Sometimes Spirit has to wait until you're unconscious to deliver the messages. Your dreams are amazing portals into your own mind. They spark imagination and wonder in us all.

Are they literal or symbolic? Are they prophetic or vague? Are they true or are they just processing through daily life?

I say, all of the above. Some dreams are just that. Run of the mill, wake up naked in class dream. Some dreams are mysterious and we want to dive deep into their meaning, picking them apart piece by piece. Those are my favorite. There are still others, dreams that carry messages. We see a lost loved one and they say our Aunt or Mother's name. They give you a message. You deliver it to the recipient.

"Dreams are illustrations...
from the book your soul is
writing about you."

~ Marsha Norman

The funny thing about dreams is they fade
quickly after we wake from sleep. When we
consciously begin processing things, our
mind has to push away what isn't needed
for day to day life, think about as closing an
app. The dream state is an app and it closes
upon walking. The system's memory (our
brain) writes over it in an attempt to
conserve space and be as efficient as
possible. Bye bye - dream memories. They

vanish nearly as soon as you sit up. We've all experienced this dream amnesia.

The easy remedy for this is to keep a dream journal near your bedside. Keep a fresh pen or pencil and write down your dreams as soon as you wake up. When the alarm goes off, hit snooze but instead of falling asleep - write down your recollections of your dreams from the night before.

I recommend drawing the symbol for the moon. A crescent or full moon, combo even, is traditional. Mercury's symbol would suit nicely too. He can help strengthen the message. Feel free to draw any other symbols on the book of your choosing. Use symbols that tap into your dream world. Like poems or quotes about dreams, write them there. Whatever gets you inspired. It isn't satanic worship to use symbols, symbols inspire the mind to react in certain ways.

Remember, the dream will be fading fast. Write down the major themes. Key characters. A plot. Snippets of dialogue, if you can recall. If not skip to Time. Place. Feeling.

Your entry may look something like this:

October 17th

I fell down from a tree.

I kept hitting branches.

Heron. Monkey. Zebra.

We talked about berries.

One was poisonous.

The other toucan ate a worm.

It was sunny. Hot. And I felt safe.

There you go. It took 30 seconds to write that. Then back to bed I went.

Understand this, remembering will get easier and easier. As you practice every morning, make a routine, you will find that your brain begins to recall more and more. You are able to tap into the dreams for longer periods and before you know it you're writing more detail, you can remember full conversations and you may even be able to recall it later in the day.

Don't let those dreams fade. They have meaning. Some are for you. They are about your personal path. Your journey and what you are completing in this life. Others will be about friends, family, your community and sometimes the world.

Did you know, millions of people reported horrifying and catastrophic dreams days before 9/11? Yes. The collective ripple from that event touched so many lives. The cosmic effect was huge! Many psychics saw it months in advance. Many reported it to authorities, that's why we have records of it.

Don't believe me? Look it up for yourself.
You will be astounded at what is out there.

Every week or once a month, go through your dream journal.
What overarching themes do you notice?
Is there a person or place that appears often?
Who are you usually talking to?
Are there any repeating dreams? (Pay close attention to those. They are usually VERY important.)
Make note of these and give the messages you receive.

"When you get, give. When you learn, teach."

-Maya Angelou

Psychic ability exists and you are on the threshold of understanding how you fit into the world of   Spirits and the divine!

CHAPTER 2

The High Priestess

She looks beyond the veil,

Her eyes clouded and pale.

The moon shines in her smile.

Her words bring wisdom's spiral.

The apple of truth is bittersweet.

Her words kind and gentle be.

Element: Air

Zodiac: Aquarius

Blessing: Intuition

Challenge: Listening

In ancient times past, before kings went
on war crusades, before the tribe moved to
hunt for the season, before people made
any decisions in their life, they sought out
the Oracle. An Oracle is a messenger of
Spirit. Forteller of the future and shamans of
old helped their people by guiding them by
casting lots, divination and by reading the
signs of Spirit written on the wall, spoken on
the wind and felt in the rain. Divination is a
time honored tradition.

Our modern world is heavily dependent upon logic. Essentially squandering the gift of intuition and the ability to divine the voice of God. Much to our detriment, if you ask me.

The High Priestess, the Oracle, asks us to trust our inner guidance. Guidance from the heart and not solely dependent on logic. Logic tries to place patterns and restrictions on the chaos of life. In a way, logic helps man find a semblance of control. But life is ruled by chaos. Rain befalls the good and falls as easily on the bad. Your tire can flatten for no reason. Your mother can get sick and die without warning. All of these happenings make us keenly aware of the chaotic balance of the universe. The seer asks us to trust that though logic can't see the pattern in the problems or events, that there is a divine connection gently guiding each of us along our path.

My friend Angie, talented psychic medium and Oracle, told me a wonderful story during my first reading with her. Her insight has been invaluable and eye opening along my journey.

Before I met her, I was scared.

I was searching for answers, that I never seemed to find. After the reading, I felt a sense of things falling into place. I found a center. I was changed. She drew an Animal Medicine Oracle card. The card she drew was Deer. Each card comes along with a teaching story for your life path.

The story of Deer Spirit is one of love.

Deer Spirit is kind, compassionate and loving. It trusts and loves when there is darkness around. It isn't afraid of the wild unknown, no it bounds forward knowing life

will catch it. Deer has the heart of a child.
An innocent.

Deer Spirit wanted to visit Creator. To do so,
Deer Spirit had to make the arduous journey
up the Sacred Mountain. At the top, Creator
set in mighty splendor. Light emanated from
the lofty peak. The trail was steep and
difficult even for Deer. Few walked the road
along beside Deer. Many coming back
seemed disheartened and ashamed. They
held their heads down in defeat.

Deer's heart began to race as she
approached the first gate.

Unbeknownst to Deer, the first gate was
guarded by the demon of Fear.

Deer watched as a spirit approached the gate. The demon of Fear jumped out and transformed into a walking nightmare. The spirit shrieked and fled back down the path.

With its heart racing, Deer knew fear. Deer is not the top of the food chain. Deer had been hunted. Chased. Killed for sport, by animal and human alike.

As Deer approached the gate, the demon of Fear jumped out and transformed into a man holding a gun to Deer's forehead.

Deer began to fear but a small voice inside said that was not the answer. Deer's fur rippled as goosebumps passed down its spine. And then it realized what would defeat the demon of Fear.

Love. Fear is the opposite of love. Fear can destroy love. However, Love can banish fear.

Deer raised its eyes to meet the demon's stare. Deer poured its heart into the gaze as its eyes locked with the demon's.

Deer sent our one thought: I love you.

The demon stepped back. It rocked on its heals and began to shutter. The demon convulsed and melted into a black puddle. Deer walked through the gate unimpeded.

The temple of the Most High allowed Deer to enter in because it conquered fear. It learned the greatest lesson.

Conquer fear and you become a champion of Love and Light! You become a beacon of Light!

The way is open to the peak of the sacred mountain because of love. You can take that further and remember an altar song that many Protestant churches sang nearly every Sunday, As The Deer.

"As the deer, panteth for the water. So my soul thirsts after thee."

The void we feel in our hearts. The void we try to bury with sex, drugs, relationships, careers, hobbies and more can only be filled with one thing - a connection to the divine. Do not give into the doctrine that Deity or

Creator is your friend. It is more than that. Creator is the highest vibration possible. It transcends our human understanding and surpasses the perception of our greatest scientific instruments.

There is one way to find Creator.
That is to seek it! Seek Creator in all you do.

If you are not, you are operating at lower vibrational levels. Your soul purpose will go unfulfilled. You will dive back into another karmic "choose your own" adventure and you will miss the point entirely!

Our souls thirst to be reunited with the God Spark! Our place of origin. Our true home!

Sin is nothing but a move in the wrong direction. If you are not following your soul path, you are in sin. Spirit sends you signs and trials to show you that you are not taking the most correct path for you. Not that you won't reach your destination eventually, you will be taking the long road.

Spirit knows the shortcut! It'll get you there with twice the time to spare!
Before we go any further, I want you to ask yourself one question.

"What do I believe in?"

Take out a pen and paper or boot up that laptop, then begin to write.
At the top, write "What do I believe in?"

Then make a list of all the things you believe in. They can be divine, they can be day to day things. The options are endless. We all believe in something.

Don't worry. You can set the book down now.
I'll be here when you get back....

Don't read ahead. That's cheating!

I wrote down God, Creator, Divinity, Peace, Love, Balance, Gratitude, Forgiveness, Grace.
I wrote many many things on my list.

One more question for you, how long did it take you to write "Myself?"

If you didn't it's okay. I didn't either. Spirit likes to catch me in my tricks! Haha! They know me so well. Spirit will point out the obvious when you've ran out of options.

I should've wrote myself first thing. I do believe in myself, but often times we forget ourselves. We are so worried about being right, or helping others find the way that we forget ourselves. If we don't believe in ourselves, then who will?

Hopefully, you are lucky like me and I have a multitude of people that believe in me. They support me and lift me up in times of distress. It is a gift from Creator that I have so many friends and family in my life. It literally took a village to raise me! Must've been adopted from wolves!

Believe in yourself! That is the lesson.

Lesson 3

In chapter 1, we talked about the path to the divine. We talked about believing in yourself. Why would those two things be important? Funny you should ask. (Don't you hate it when authors ask questions and then answer themselves?!)

I wanted you to realize how important you are. There is nothing like you. Nothing like you has ever occurred and nothing will again! Of all the millions of choices and opportunities that were taken to lead right to this moment in time, for you to be reading this book, is monumental. Albert Einstein couldn't equate that formula! But someone did!

You!

You chose this moment! Right here, right now to begin something new. To start a journey with me.

Seekers to the Temple of Delphi in ancient Greece were greeted with 2 words before they knelt at the altar of the seer. Before they could see their future, before power of time itself was bestowed in their hands, the gatekeeper appeared. It came as words written on the wall, above the threshold of the temple, it said,

Μάθε τον εαυτό σου
"Know Thyself."

As a Shaman, I am intimately involved in the human experience. To know my clients is to know myself. Each client reflects back a different part or aspect of who I am. Their fears are my fears. Their hate is my hate. Their pain is my pain. Their love is my love. I am the Walker Between Worlds. Having walked darker roads by night than most would dare to walk in the noon sun, I have become accustomed to the ups and downs of life. Its pitfalls. Its snares. Its danger. The Other World mirrors the Physical Realm after all. "As above, So Below" isn't just a t-shirt motto. The traditional meaning of shaman is One Who Sees in the Dark. I see into situations because I can bend my perception of it. Time is relative. Soul wounds can carry bleeding wounds for decades. The soul doesn't heal like the body does, but the body is a reflection of the soul.

Know Thyself.

Why are those words so important? You're greatest fear is also your greatest strength

Your weakness is what makes you stronger.

As Rumi said, "The wound is the place where the Light enters in."
The Dark will always try to use that fear or weakness against you. When you know your greatest fear. It then becomes a weapon! You will not be tempted by the Dark anymore. It will have no hold over your heart!

Take a moment to quiet your mind. Center yourself.

To Center is to connect with the universe. As above, so be

lo

w. You create sacred Axis Mundi, you become the center of the world.

MERKABAH

Lay down or sit in a comfortable position.
Relax your body and breathe deeply in for a
count 3. Breathe out for count of 4.
Move your awareness to your hips.
From your Root Chakra (the womb or the
prostate) create 4 white spheres. Place
them in 3 corners around you.
See a white line of light drawn from your
center to the 3 spheres.
While holding that image, create 3 more
white spheres in between the previous
spheres.
With those spheres connected to your Root,
see another line of light connect to a sphere
below your feet and one above your head.
You have created a sacred merkabah.

The heart of the universe.

Fill the merkaba with white light.

You feel energy pulsating up the white lines of light from each sphere, below you the strength and protection of Earth. Above you comes energy from the divine and peace of the cosmos.

You are now Centered and Grounded.

When you are ready release the energy to flow where it needs to go.

If you feel like you are buzzing or light headed and dizzy, place your hands on the ground palms down and release the remaining energy to Gaia.

What do you see?

What do you feel?

What do you hear?

Not with you outward senses but within.

Can you taste anything?

Spirit speaks to us in different ways.

Learn your light language.

Lesson 4

The Silent Witness

Now that you can create sacred space and center yourself - you are ready to do most anything! Play around! Have fun with it! The world is your oyster, as they say.

But one little ingredient is missing.

In Lesson 3, we talked about the Silent Witness. We will connect the inner thoughts to the Silwnt Witness. This process is part of harnessing your will.

From day to day, our minds are pulled in several different directions. We shoot this way and that. A select few remain balanced and centered. Some can do this naturally without any training. For the rest of us, myself included, we have to cultivate moments that allow us to return to center. The Shamanic Journey is a perfect way to get in touch with this heart of stone, inner peace and harmony in the chaos.

For the next exercise we will journey not outward, but inward. Remember, As Above, So Below. When you learn to journey inward, you are also creating a means to journey outward. It is all connected.

You stand in sovereignty and grace because we are all connected. All life is woven tightly together like an exquisite tapestry. We only perceive the smallest parts of it through our sight and perception. But what if I told you, you could follow a thread to its source? Or to another thread and space entirely?

You can! It's as easy as breathing.

The Shamanic Journey is an energetic state that we achieve on a daily basis. When you're zoned out watching TV that is the energetic state you should be in to journey. When you have a lapse in memory while driving, that hypnagogic state is similar to the conscious level you are attempting to reach. There are deeper and deeper states. I would wager science hasn't even begun to understand the possibilities.

Working in nursing homes and from anecdotal stories, we know that patients in comas can hear and understand the conversations, emotions and even sounds happening in the room. Some say they could see it from above, a bird's eye view. Others just heard it or saw what was happening. We are all unique and each brain is unique. Your frequency and DNA combined creates your special set of gifts.

There are 4 major

Spi

ritual Gifts:

Clairvoyance- Clairvoyance is the ability of inner sight. This ability is the one most often portrayed in Hollywood movies and films. Although it may not appear like a movie. It can be pictures. Or drawings. Or colors or numbers and symbols.

Clairaudience- Clairaudience is the ability of inner hearing. This ability allows the wielder to pick up sounds that aren't heard in 3d reality. Voices. Words. Even conversations sometimes come through. If you've ever heard your name called out but no one was there, you are clairaudient.

Clairsentience- Clairsentient is the ability of inner feelings, emotions or physical manifestations. Empaths are Clairsentient. They pick up on feelings and emotions that sometimes grow into full blown physiological reactions. Goosebumps or the hair standing on end is Clairsentience.

Claircognizance- Claircognizance is the ability of inner knowing. This ability allows ideas, thoughts and concepts to be downloaded into your memory. You just know. Have you ever known exactly how many beans were in the jar at the fair? Have you ever known someone was in trouble, not a feeling but an internal alert? That is claircognizant.

The four major psychic gifts can be mixed in any combination. If you are not good at one, try another. Ability and finesse should not be confused. I am clairvoyant, clairsentient and claircognizant. I rarely hear messages. But words and phrases pop up. With practice, I could tune into my inner inner ear. Just as you can boost your clairvoyance if it is not your strongest gift. They are muscles. Work with them and they grow. Also, depending on the experience and atmosphere, Spirit may chose completely uncharted or different ways to communicate with you.

One day you could hear messages all day long, from the radio, from friends and your inner inner ear then the next you have snapshots of places and people you don't know. Spirit can use any method that is best for reaching your attention.

For now, stick with the one you believe is your strong suit. For me, that is clairvoyance. So visualization works wonders for me. I see vivid pictures and panoramas in my head. It's my favorite as its traditional and I love the ride it takes me on. For you, you may love to talk. Listen to spirit. Start up that dialogue. Act like you're talking to an old friend. Catch up.

Reminisce. For my Claircognizant readers, automatic writing is your best friend. You write a question or write out the journey like a story. Just write. Let go of expectations and create a stream of consciousness. Soon you'll be tapping into your inner knowing with ease.

I say this in preparation for our first outing into the Spirit Realm. It's time for a field trip! We've studied. We've practiced. Now it's time to explore! The best experience is experience!
It's time to experience Spirit.

Find a quiet place where you will not be disturbed for 20 minutes or more.

Have your pen and paper nearby. Gather any sacred items you wish. Perhaps some Amethyst to help ground and free the mind. Maybe a Lapis Lazuli to open up communication between this world and the hidden worlds. Some sage to cleanse the area of negativity. And your best self. If you have any burdens, leave them at the door. Relax into yourself. Be you for a few moments. Not Mom. Not Uncle. Not Boss. Not Coach. Not Grocery Cashier. Not Barhop.

Just you.

Shed the masks you wear. You're entering the halls of truth. Your illusions won't hold up here. You will come as you are.

Take a moment to create sacred space. Following the steps in Exercise 3, allow your mood to shift from every day to one of ceremony and magic.

Settle into the center. For this exercise I would sit or lie down facing the West, direction of Water and the Heart. We will be journeying inward. Water will help ease the transition.

You may set a timer for 20 minutes. It might help to record the steps on your phone or with a tape recorder, that way you can follow along and not have to read.

Play some soft music, if you feel led. I'm a musical person, I love it as a theme song for life. But when I meditate or journey, I prefer silence. It feels right to me. No distractions. Just me.

Close your eyes.

With your eyes closed, begin to create a picture in your mind. I use the image of a Silver Screen. It is opaque and silver, almost like a mirror. Very similar to a modern television but huge like at the movie theater so it reaches the edges of my field of vision.

On the screen I see the number 12.

As the numbers begin to descend, I feel each one pull me deeper inward. I allow my body to relax. I allow my consciousness to move inward. You have all done this, shifting your consciousness. Have you ever stubbed your toe? All of your awareness shoots to your big toe, right? Shifting your awareness inward is the same. Well, less traumatic than the toe incident but the idea is similar. In good health, allow your awareness to go deep with you. Many teachers use breath to teach this descent. Breathe in and focus on the breath. The intent is to be drawn inward with each breath and stay there as you watch the exhale.

With each descending number, 11.
With each breath, 10.
You become more relaxed, 9.
Your body becomes still, 8.
Your muscles from your head, 7.

Down your spine, 6.

To the tips of your toes, 5.

Relax. 4

Deeper still. 3.

Breathe in. 2.

Breathe out. 1

On the next breath, look at the inner screen. Watch as it begins to shimmer and ripple like a pond. You can see it is a doorway now. A portal to the Other World.

Step through it. Like Alice stepping through the looking glass, allow imagery from the Matrix and Alice to help you experience the shift.

Step inward.

On the other side is a path. Follow the path as it borrows downward. Now.

Look up. Do you see the world above you? You're seated above. Thoughts still race about in your head but you are below it. You mat be able to faintly hear them but they aren't right up in your face anymore. They are distant. They are just leaves on the breeze. Nothing more.

In front of you is a seat. In that seat sets your Silent Witness.

What do you look like? Is it your Inner Child? Is it you in your full radiant, glory? Are you male or female? Are you neither?

Take a moment to introduce yourself. You are meeting a critical part of who you are. Your Silent Witness is the gatekeeper between your conscious mind and your unconscious mind. It is the interpreter for two systems that don't speak the same language. It's like the person at the airport, the ground control that uses lit beacons to signal plans how to land and where to go from there to avoid collisions and chaos. Your Silent Witness is mediator.

Take a moment and sit awhile with yourself. The conversation may stretch on into silence. That's okay. Just be. Remember this feeling. You can return here anytime to avoid the chaos above.
The conversation be so stimulating that you begin writing it all down. Either way,

whatever experience you have is authentic and perfectly true for your journey and purpose now.

Thank your Silent Witness for meeting you today. We will journey back again and again to this place. It is the launching pad to greater mysteries.

Return the way you came. Find the shifting surface of the movie screen and walk back through it.

See the number 1 appear on the screen. As it ascends, feel yourself slip back into reality, 2.
Wiggle your toes, 3.
Flex your leg muscles, 4.
Feel your breath stretch your torso, 5.

Roll your shoulders gently, 6.

Move your neck from side to side, 7.

Gently roll your head around, 8.

Breathe in, 9.

Breathe out, 10.

You are fully engaged here and now, 11.

Welcome back, 12.

Open your eyes and yawn or stretch.

Whatever feels natural.

You have completed your first journey. You may release your circle or you may leave it to fade as it wishes. Either is fine.

Write about your journey in your notes. Over the next few weeks, I would practice this journey 3 times a week. Sunday, Tuesday, Friday. Monday, Wednesday, Friday. It doesn't matter to me. Whatever works for you schedule but make a promise to yourself and to your path that you will do the work. Reading the boom and kot doing the exercises is totally fine. But it's kinda like going to the gym for the music. You are missing the experience. Take a leap of faith and try it out.

If visualization is not your forte, then give automatic writing a try.

Write out the journey instead of seeing it. When you write out questions for your Silent Witness, listen and wait for answers, ideas or thoughts to pop into your head then write them down. It works exactly the same. One is not better than the other. It's a different way of seeing, that's all.

We are all so unique. We are all made perfectly as we are. There's a part for every voice in the choir. You only have to learn where you belong. Trying to sing out of your range can be frustrating, not impossible but frustrating. Start easy. If you know you're more clairvoyant, start with the visualization then work your way up to automatic writing. Maybe you can combine the two! Play with it! The tools are just that, tools. It's how you use them that makes you unique.

Practice this exercise for at least a week before moving on to chapter 2. It is the cornerstone of journey work and healing. Tap into your ability. Learn how you fly. In the next chapter, we will prepare to soar!

Lesson 6

Automatic Writing

Writing is a tried and true method of communicating with Spirit. All of us learn to write at a young age. In fact, if you break down the word "write", have writ or rite, the first is a law or command, the latter is a right of passage or solemn ceremony. When you "write" you are taking part in something sacred.

Many years ago, the church did not want peasants to be literate or possess the ability to write above common numbers for sums and maybe a person's name. That was the extent of the education given to millions. It was to keep the flock dumb. Keep the sheep in line and choraled.

The Burning Times wasn't just about burning witches and warlocks. No, it was about burning hundreds upon thousands of volumes of esoteric and occult knowledge that did not coincide with the teachings of the church. Much of our very history and lore, stories that would reshape history were lost to the fires. It was a great purging and a mighty blow to humanity.

Remember this each time you pick up a pen and paper or type out a message. Enter a state of gratitude that you can freely express yourself and your ideas in this way.

It is sacred.

Let's not forget that.

Maybe we wouldn't have so much hate spewed on social media and the internet if we recalled how far we fell when we lost control. How far we stumbled when we let one group decide what was right and what was not. Lest we repeat history.

The reason I want to instill the importance of writing and its spiritual component is to move into a mindset that will help you when you practice Automatic Writing. The practice of Automatic Writing is not new. It was practiced early on in the human experience. Priests and mystics have channeled Spirit through the written word throughout the millennia.

Automatic writing is simple. The only tools you will need are a writing utensil, some paper (I prefer a notebook so I can flip pages quickly without breaking the rhythm), and an open mind. It's really that easy!

The best way to get results is to create a routine or a ritual. We have hectic lives with work, school or play. Some of you have children and they take up much of your time and attention. Creating a routine to follow will help you and your family learn when you need time to work together and when you need space to work on yourself.

Begin the exercise in a quiet place where you will not be disturbed for at least 30 minutes. Create an atmosphere of sacredness. Turn on some soothing music, preferably with little or no words. You don't want the lyrics to unconsciously seep into your writing. It can happen!

Light some incense or diffuse an oil to stimulate the mind. You will want your mind sharp and ready to take flight. Good essential oils for this are:

Rosemary

Basil

Cypress (my fav choice)

Peppermint

Sage or Clary Sage

Feel free to play around with different aromas and blends. Find one that helps your mind stay sharp but also evokes mystical experience and exotic notes. I love Cypress for this purpose. It's one of my "go-to" oils. Cypress is elemental fire, it helps with will power and passion. It's a lively, sharp scent.

Sidenote:

Long ago, in the Temple of Delphi, the Sybil would sit in a cave surrounded by the beast, Python's vapors. The temple itself had a long walkway lined with Cypress trees, the trees were held sacred by Apollo. Sybil was blessed by the God, Apollo - chariot driver of the Sun, illuminator of esoteric mysteries and god of healing and prophecy. The Sybil would chew on cypress leaves to induce a trance. From within her trance, the Sybil would prophesy for seekers. She would tell them of visions of luck or misfortune. She would simply relate what the God Apollo showed her.

I like to use Cypress oil to evoke that place and time. Its sharp scent hits my nose and I'm transported back to the days of old where the veil was thinner and gods walked among men. Use something that stimulates your imagination, after all, Spirit dwells in the innermost corners of our minds. Spirit's words are our thoughts. Spirit's sight is our day dream or vision.

Now that you have prepared your area. Use the steps in Lesson 3, Creating Sacred Space, to dispel any negative energy from your chosen space and to further ready your body and mind to intercede with Spirit. It helps set a frame of mind of ritual when you're seeking messages from the divine. We are suckers for the dramatic, aren't we? It is not necessary, but it helps stimulate something primal within us.

Sit quietly for a moment. Clear your mind and let the stresses and worries of the day fade away. Just for a moment. Find your center. Practice breath work. Inhale deeply. And exhale slowly and with purpose. Allow your awareness to spiral down to your core.

Once you feel ready. Begin to write.

Write what you feel. Write what you hear. Write what you smell. Reach out with your senses. What images do you see within your mind?

Write it all down. You may start writing in rhyme. Or you may just write gibberish. It is okay. Keep writing.

At first, it may be all over the place. You may write about a mountain stream one moment and then about a yellow car the next. Go with the flow. Follow where your mind, body and all of your senses take you. You are acting as a radio right now. You are tuning into frequencies and messages written on the air, whispered in the wind, scented on the breeze.

Let it flow.

You may want to just practice this stream of consciousness a few times to get the hang of it. Don't be discouraged if you feel silly. It is silly. You're sitting alone writing whatever pops into your head. But don't lose hope. You are tapping into Spirit. When you go back through and read what you wrote, you will find patterns, words you don't remember writing and messages that will jump out at you.

Though you have cleared your mind, if your mind wonders that is okay. You may start thinking about your sister or brother. Then you'll start wondering if they're okay. What are they up to? You are sending out an intent. You are formulating a question. As you write, you will find all or some of your questions were answered. Just keep writing.

Practice:
Automatic writing with intent
Note- The exercise will have you connect with a friend or family member, please get permission first. Free will is a real thing. It

exists in our plane, try not to pry into people's lives without consent.

Begin your session as usual. Create sacred space, ready your notepad and pen, and begin to relax. Clear your mind and spiral down to your center.

"They spiral down into ebony, catching the stars with their tails."
-Anne Bishop, The Black Jewels Trilogy

Once you feel comfortable and in the right state of mind, focus your mind on a friend, a family member or a loved one. Hold their image in your mind. When you can see them clearly or feel their presence, begin to ask questions about them.
What are they doing?

What color is their shirt?

What did they have for breakfast?

What mood are they in?

What are they worried about?

Once you have asked the questions and then written down your intuitive answers. Call them up. And ask them to answer the questions you asked yourself and Spirit.

Compare the answers.

You will be astounded how accurate the readings will be! I'm still amazed at my insight. But, I remind myself, it's not me. Its Spirit! Spirit is amazing and loves to WOW me on a daily basis.

Chapter 3

The Empress

She walks along the banks of the river,
Her crown of stars shine and glitter.

Golden scepter in her right hand, Dominion over sea and land.

Abundance and fertility, Harmony and prosperity.

Feel her embrace and warm by her fire.

Feel your deepest longings, heart's true desires.

Element: Water

Zodiac: Pisces

Blessing: Abundance

Challenge: Gluttony

Abundance and Prosperity is one of the main goals clients have in mind when they seek me out. They want to know the perfect job that will align with their true selves and make money. They need insight on where their money is going and how to handle it wisely. Spirit gives and Spirit takes away.

The human race has become enslaved to the coin of the era. The Dollar. The Yen. The Pound. The Euro. Money has enslaved humanity. We live in constant fear and isolation from one another because we become misers or dragons of old guarding our golden treasure.

Monies energy is liquid. Fluid. Money will travel to the place of least resistance. But most of it is dammed up in a circle of corporations, grant's and taxes. Our nourishment has literally been siphoned away from us -The People - and into the hands of the few. The "water of life" is hoarded by the few.

The key to abundance and living a prosperous life is not finding buried treasure or riches untold, but simply a mindset of gratitude. The universe works by way of the Law of Attraction. Like calls to like. When we think negative thoughts, "I am unlovable," "I wish I was rich," "I need to get out of this job." The universe hears only "unlovable, poverty and work." When we only pray for wants and needs the universe sees us as lacking. The universe hesitates to send us more because we are not content with what we have.
Simple right?

Think about it like this.

If you are an employer and you're trying to decide who to promote. Are you going to promote the one who needs help all the time, is always late, can't seem to utilize their time and tools of the trade wisely? Or an employee who does their best without supervision, is always on time and doesn't need extra tools or help to get the job done?

Obviously you would promote the latter.

Gratitude works the same. My Grandmom, a wise sage of a woman, has a saying that she picked up while reading the Bible.

"No matter the circumstances I find myself in, I will be content."

The phrase is from Philippians 4:11. Paul wrote this book of the Bible to the church in

Philippi during his imprisonment in Rome. Wrap your mind around that for a moment.

Philippians is hailed as one of the most joyful and thankful books of the Bible and it was written in a prison cell. Not once does Paul mention the state of his imprisonment, he's not talking about his treatment, instead he rejoices that Spirit is using him even in his bondage. Now here is a man who understood Gratitude.

The other part of Gratitude is not only having a joyful attitude but being thankful for what you are given. That is just proper manners. Everyone expects a 'Thank you' when we give something to someone. Spirit is no different. As Above, So Below. If someone can make us happy by a simple thank you, then Spirit is the same. Thank you is a positive energy exchange. Gratefulness balances out the scales. The gift may be freely given but gratefulness warms the heart. Let's feel the world with gratitude and watch the world change one heart at a time. It would catch like a wildfire! Spreading virally around the world!

The Law of Attraction can make you or break you. The energy can keep you chained to a life of poverty and need or it can free you from your chains and set you free. Your wildest dreams are possible when you let go of the indoctrinated idea of prayer and say what you mean.

The trick is using positive affirmations or statements.

"I need money" becomes "I have money."

"Nobody loves me" becomes "I am loved."

"I'm not good enough" becomes "I am worthy."

Do you see the pattern. Take your desire and place it after an "I am" statement.

Practice gratitude and positive affirmations. Reverse the flow of the resources. Bring the nourishment back to the people.

Thank you!

Lesson 5:

Ancestral Fire

***Read through this entire exercise before performing the ritual.

Take a few moments to gather your thoughts.

What do you want to do with your life?

Who are you deep down inside?

What do you truly want?

Take a piece of paper and write down your affirmations.

"I release all pain and suffering, I choose love and happiness from this day forward."

"I am filled with abundance and prosperity. I will rise above like never before!"

"I am loved. I am worthy! I am forgiven. The past has no hold on me and I turn towards a brighter future."

Make the list as long or short as you need.

I used Red and Blue ink, symbols of freedom and love, dedication and loyalty.

Now, go outside, ask Mother Earth to bless your work. Create a fire pit by digging a 3ft x 3ft hole and lining it with rocks or use an existing fire pit. I have used an existing fire and I have made a fire pit. Both work well for this exercise.

Walk around in a wooded area, pick up wood that is given to you. I found black walnut, mulberry, hickory and cedar. Place some newspaper or kindling at the bottom of the pit and then set up your wood in a small pyramid. Then keep adding wood in a triangular formation until you have placed every piece with intent and care.

Light the fire!

As the flames rise, feel your Spirit catch flame alongside the tender. Open your heart. Put out your feelers to taste the air, feel the sunshine or moonlight on your skin. Listen to the crackle of the fire, listen to the wind rustling through the trees. You are present. You are in this moment.

The sacral fire rises in unison with the external fire! You catch flame with passion and desire to manifest your will.

For a moment just be. Sing. Dance. Move. Really enjoy this moment and time in your physical body as we release all the tension that we harbor there.

Forget about the past. Don't worry about the future. Just be for a moment. Breathe deeply and slowly spiral down to your core.

As the flames catch and cast their hypnotic light around you, feel the air shift.

Use the exercise in chapter 1 to create sacred space. Call the elements. Call the energies to hold the circle in place.

Additionally, call to your ancestors. Call to Spirit to be with you as you awaken your eternal fire.

Take out your list and read it aloud to yourself and to the Spirits gathered with you.

Say each word strongly and with emotion. You've got to mean it!

Then place the page on the flames. Let the fire cleanse and transmute the body of your work. Be set free! The chains of the past melt away as the page is taken by the flame.

Sit and meditate with Spirit. Take a pen and paper. Watch the flames and write down your perceptions. Thoughts, visions, feelings, scents and ideas. Write them down. Feel the flames shine light on the dark regions of your mind. Write down what you discover.

After a while, make an offering to Spirits, Ancestors and other beings that came to your aid. I place a cake or berries or pour some wine on the flames. (Note: Be careful pouring any alcoholic beverage on a flame. They are highly flammable. Use caution and common sense.)

After the fire has gone down, make sure that it burns itself out completely. Stay with it the entire time. Watch the kindling as it decays in flames. What portends are hidden in the dying embers?

Write down your final messages and perceptions. Thank Spirit for communing with you and awakening your sacral fire.

Remember this feeling when times are hard. Light that inner fire. You have done it once. It will be easier from this moment on to light your fire again.

In a few hours or the next day, collect a small bit of the ashes. Place them in a bag and keep this with you for the future. Place it in your medicine bag for power or carry it in your pocket on days when you need some pep in you step.

Lesson 6:

We are all connected

Empathy is the greatest magick tool we naturally all possess. Empathy allows us to walk a mile in someone's shoes. Some of us have disconnected from that natural gift. It is there. Only a heartbeat away.

Each heart is made of similar material. Muscle, cells, membranes and veins. The law of attraction makes our hearts connected whether we perceive the link or not. The hug is a lost ritual of connecting heart to heart.

The next time you hug someone, place your head towards their left shoulder. Feel the difference as your hearts meet for a brief moment. You just connected to their energy.

I warn every client that walks through my door, "Imma hugger!" before I wrap them in a big bear hug. I want to connect with them intimately. Pirates energies align in that brief moment. I get insights and discoveries from that fleeting link alone. As I work on them with visualization and hands on healing, more and more of their layers of defense, conditioning and mental blocks fade away and I can see the real person underneath. Some would say, I see their very soul.

The heart is the mediator between the spiritual and the physical. Our brains act as the third wheel that translates those perceptions, insights and feelings through our mouth and words.

We are not the mind. We are the heart and soul. Deep down underneath the layers that have been applied or we have applied, that is our true selves.

Find a partner. This can be someone you know or someone you work with or just an acquaintance.

Invite them over for a chance to unburden and discover more about who they are. When they arrive, embrace them. Make sure when you hug that your head moves to their left side. That might be awkward at first. But new things always do. You may not always hug this way but you will grow to appreciate the connection.

When you embrace, close your eyes and scan your body, take note of any fleeting thoughts, emotions or even smells. What taste is in your mouth? Obviously, if you had coffee earlier and all you taste is coffee - disregard. We know why that flavor is there. :)

Now sit down with them. Offer them a glass of water or something to nibble on. And talk to them.

Ask them how they are doing.

What's going on in their lives?

How is work?

Be their friend in truth.

We have forgotten this connection in our social media world. We think we know everyone's business and everyone's truth but through artificial means. We couldn't be more disconnected by trading organic interaction for a few keyswipes.

On a piece of paper or in your mind, take not of any insights that come through. How do you feel when they talk about their partner? What emotions or pains arise when they talk about their job? Do you get a bad taste in your mouth when they talk about their grandparents?

Jot down the revelations. Don't force it. Don't disregard anything at first. Let the information flow freely through you and within you.

Listening is so much more than paying attention. Listening is honoring your responses in your body and mind. The images that surface in their presence may be a message they need to heed. Don't formulate your responses before they are finished speaking. Open up and truly listen. It is a lost art.

We wonder why our elders are so wise. They have learned to listen and THEN respond. In our fast paced world, we are worried about being witty or clever and we start formulation our response before the speaker is even finished talking. Wait.

Relax. And let go of that programming. It's old, outdated and a waste of time.

You're missing the point entirely. Let go of that ego self and hear and feel what they are telling you.

At the end of your conversation, discuss your findings with them.
For example:

"Why did my back hurt when you were talking about your job? Does it ever hurt during your work day? What are you doing to cause this? Avoid that."

"I smelled smoke when you talked about your Grandfather. Was he a smoker? How are his lungs?"

"My blood ran cold when you talked about your boss. Are you afraid of him or her?"

Examples like this are the purest form of connection. Empathy. Their heart is speaking directly to your heart. You are actually being "psychic."

My firm belief is that, in this golden age, we are all psychic. We were all born with gifts. No man is an island. We are connected. By the energy that flows through us all. Light calls every single one of us. And so many of us are waking up to the idea that we may be more perceptive than we ever dreamed possible.

There is no limit to what you can discover.

Only the limitation of your own mind. Let it go and let the ego fall away.

You choose!

Chapter 4:

The Emperor

Long he sits in throne of stone,

A silent sentinel guards the bone.

Fire shimmers in his eyes.

Hardened and stoic is his guise.

Rule the kingdom just and fair.

Live thy life without a care.

Element: Fire

Zodiac: Aries

Blessing: Ownership

Challenge: Power

Magic is All Around You

Folklore and myth harken back to a time
when men battled monsters, beasts of
legend and the gods roamed the Earth. Man

had to rise up and face adversity. Choose greatness and love for fellow man over love of self. Or be crushed by the atrocities of the age.

There were two types of people. The first, the witness, the witness sat by and watched the world simply a spectator.

We have walked through the journey of the witness. Now we must understand the second archetype: The Hero

The hero does not stand by and watch others suffer. No - the hero rises above the circumstance and hurls a javelin in the giants eye. In many circumstances, being the witness is safe and right. But some of us, at times and with the right opportunities will rise up and become heroes.

The hero stands for justice. The hero stands for balance. The chaos of the universe is reigned in by the hero.

In Egyptian Mythology, we learn the story of Set. Set is more like the anti-hero. He kills his brother, Osiris. Chops up his remains and throws them into the Underworld. They scatter in the wind. Set leaves Isis, his brothers wife, tearfully searching for his body parts in the bowels of hell.

Head.

Arms and hands.

Torso.

Genitals.

Legs and feet.

Isis has to pass through nine gates in search of her beloved.

Wearily she trudges day and night. Tears of blood fall down her face. Demons and monsters rip at her flesh but steady onward she marches.

We have all been through hell. Or you will on the path of Light. There is a saying that echoes truly with this passage, this initiation into power, the journey of the broken road, the dark night of the soul.

"It is always darkest before the dawn."

As you turn towards the Light, darkness will rise up to meet you. Relationships that have been solid before will crumble and test your mettle. Jobs will no longer give you joy. The house and debt will seem more like a ball and chain instead of peace. Spirit is not going to just give power away.

In every society, there is an exchange for a service or product. Spirit is no different. You must have a heart that is true and not soft or brittle.

The invitation is where many fail. Many give up, surrender their power or just take what they have learned so far and sit on the sidelines.

No! I tell you - Don't stop!

The only way out is through!

Do you know what it takes to keep placing one foot in front of the other through initiation and trials that arise?

Passion!

Fire!

Get in touch with your inner fire! Awaken the soul!

Lesson 7:
Follow the Drums Inside

Supplies:

Music or Drum or Rattle

Offering for Spirit

One of the greatest gifts I can give my clients is restoring their power back. As we go throughout our day to day lives, we are bombarded by energetic vampires, cords are attached and begin siphoning our energy. Negative vibes and frequencies crash into our energy field constantly. We are left unprotected and highly susceptible to energy and power loss.

My clients come to me exhausted and weary. They have a bone deep tiredness that is threatening to put out their fire all together. The easiest way to restore power back is to return their power.

I do this by journeying to find their power animal. Power Animals are a totem that resides within our spirit. Think of it as the animal essence of who you are. Some people have raven spirit, others the badger or the serpent spirit or the dolphin. Each animal spirit has its own lesson and gifts that they bestow on the bearer.

For example, an owl spirit person is wise and has keen sight for seeing the best line of attack or night vision. Someone who has squirrel as their power animal may be a bit scattered but very energetic and clever with their resources.

The journey is a simple one.

You will need about 30 minutes of undisturbed quiet time.

You can search the web or YouTube for a drumming or rattling piece of traditional Native American music. I would avoid any music with chanting at this time as that can distract you. You want to listen to your inner voice.

When you are ready, begin to play the music. If you have your own rattle or drum, begin a steady beat around 120 bpm. That is the traditional pace of shamanic journey accompaniment.

The shamanic path leans towards an ecstatic experience. Unlike the quiet meditations we have done so far, the journey in this exercise may be a bit lively. So free yourself up. Get limber and stretched.

Create sacred space as I taught you in lesson 1.

The journey you are about to take is a powerful one. Take every precaution to protect and cleanse the space of any negativity. Use sage and any crystals that call to you.

Ground and Center with the Merkabah configuration found in Lesson 3.

Lay down on your back or sit in a comfortable position to hold your rattle or drum. Continue to keep a steady beat or tune into the rhythm of the music you've prepared.

Allow your mind to drift on the beat. Feel your body deepen into relaxation with each beat of the drum. The drum becomes your vessel pulling you downward.

Again see the screen in your mind and perform the countdown sequence from 12 to 1.

Step through the screen and onto the path ahead. Feel the warm ground beneath you. See the dappled sunlight peeking through the trees. Here the wind rustling around the grove.

Continue on the path. As you do, the forest opens onto a valley. In the valley is the Tree of Life. Walk towards the tree.

The Shamanic Cosmos

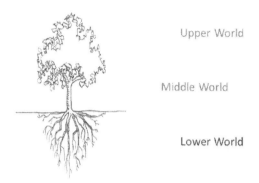

Upper World

Middle World

Lower World

In its roots you will find an opening like a cave leading downward. Take the path and enter into the Lower World. The Lower World holds the primordial beginnings of all creation.

When you come out of the tunnel, you will be greeted by an ancient forest. There is a

164

well trod path before you. Follow it to the edge of the forest.

Before you enter the Wild Wood. Call out to your power animal.

"Power Animal. My Primal Self. I call you home. Come back to be me and be known to me!"

Follow the path into the Wild Wood. As you walk pay attention to what animals you see. Traditionally, an animal that you encounter 3 times on this journey is yours.

You may see it flying or walking in the woods. Follow it! You will know which one to follow. If you don't feel it pay attention to the one which is trying to catch your eye. The one you see more than once. You called to your power animal - it is coming home, it is seeking you as you seek it.

Call once more.

"My power animal familiar to me and I to you! Come to me!"

But animals are shy of humans by nature. Don't run to the first animal you see. Keep your eyes open. Be aware of your surroundings and continue to walk down the path.

You will eventually come to a clearing or a grove. There will be a bench or seat of some kind in the center. Go to the seat. Sit down and rest a bit. We've journeyed long and far.

Call out one final time.

"Power Animal! I know you. Come to me so I might commune and be with you in this life."

Your power animal will come. Be patient and remain where you are. You will know when your power animal has come. Smile and accept your animal.

Be gentle and calm. Introduce yourself and be respectful. Your power animal will need to get to know you the same way you do any stranger. You will sense a familiarity but you may have forgotten long ago who they were and they waited a long time for you.

The most important information to glean is their name. Ask kindly and politely. Some do not have names but prefer simply 'Bear.' Either is well and good.

When you are finished thank them and offer your offering to them. They will accept in a manner that suits the occasion. Ask your Power animal to return with you to the world tree.

Your power animal will guide you and protect you as you journey back home. Once you are at the world tree, ask your Power Animal to remain with you always. You will continue to nurture the relationship and in return they care for your body during journeys and protect you in the astral as you travel.

Thank them and continue back towards the screen.

Thank deity. Release the circle and give your offering to nature. Either in your yard, in a wooded area or a river, if your particular spirit is a water creature.

Be sure to drink some water and nibble a bite to eat so you can return to your body fully.

Like the Emperors of old, we must sometimes speak with our advisors. The guide you met in the last lesson will speak to you constantly. Your power animal is your protector, companion and council. In times of need you can speak to them quickly through the use of the pendulum.

Automatic writing is great for communicating with angels, spirits of the dead, deity or other humanoid beings. Animal spirits may

not have ever been in a humanoid form.
They may not understand how to write.

I asked my power animal to channel through
me via automatic writing once and she
clocked her head to the side adorably. Then
shook her head. A strong no. Laughter
bubbled up in my head. Her mouth parted in
a sly smile and she said, "How will I hold the
pen?" We both laughed at that.

Power animals and some other beings
prefer to work with pendulums. Writing has
to be filter through many muscles and brain
goop to be distilled down to the paper. The
pendulum swings by muscle testing alone.
Your brain automatically picks up the signal
from spirit and channels it down your arm.
Remember, Spirit is like electricity and

prefers the path of least resistance. Spirit is nothing but energy, after all.

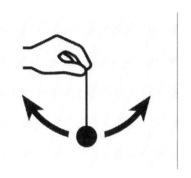

Lesson 8:

The Pendulum Sways

Many of the pieces of Osiris were scattered far and wide in the underworld. Isis paused

several time pauses several time. She
would quiet her mind and go within.
"Where are you, my beloved?" Only silence
greeted her.
No answer.
She did not despair. She did not give in to
fear.

Instead she plucked a hair from her head
and removed her wedding band. Lapis
lazuli, a stone sacred and precious to her.
Lapis is a stone of both the Throat and Third
Eye Chakra. Its bands of dark and light blue
resonate with mental energies of Air.
Psychic ability and speaking truth is
enhanced when this stone is held.

She held the pendulum in her left hand and
followed the pull of her beloved one's spirit.

Fire awakens us. Its warmth radiates inward and ripples back out as cosmic light and energy. The next element we will work with is Air. Air is in a constant state of motion. Similar to our minds, the dominion of Air, we can tap into inner knowing by utilizing our connection to our intuition.

There are many ways to do this. Scrying, meditation, journeys, divination - the list goes on and on. In this lesson, we will discuss scrying with a pendulum.

A simple pendulum can be created from a string tied around a nut. Simple as that! Some prefer to use a lock of hair around a precious ring, while others hunt esoteric shops for the perfect partner. Whichever you choose is up to you. You can even use a necklace! Anything that you can hold in your hand that will swing. A rope and rock. A cord and a stick. The possibilities are endless.

My pendulum was gifted to me by a dear friend, Heather Brownstone. Heather is a High Priestess with abilities that boggle my mind at times. I was wanting a pendulum and put the thought out there into the ether and Voila! The next day she gifted me the one that I use to this day.

The pendulum is actually a necklace. It has a silver chain with a beautiful piece of Lapis Lazuli carved into a pentagram - the modern shape of the 5 pointed star. I love that mine is made out of Lapis Lazuli! The stone reminds me of Cleopatra's eyes, her dark blue shadow was made of crushed Lapis and patted on. L. Lazuli is also a third eye stone. The third eye is responsible for "seeing." Many "clair"- abilities are associated with the third eye chakra. L. Lazuli stimulates the third eye to open and be receptive to divine messages from Spirit.

Note: You *may skip Part 1 if* *you like. I prefer ritual and ceremony around items I will use to channel Spirit. The choice is yours.* You can skip to Part 2 of this lesson.

Part 1:

Before using a pendulum, it is my routine to cleanse, bless and consecrate the pendulum to align the pendulum with my energy and intent. To cleanse, run under running water. To do this you can place the pendulum in a bag and tie it to a stick and set it in running water that is dear to you, like a favorite river or creek. Running it under a faucet will have the same affect. (WARNING- Look up the type of crystal your pendulum is fashioned from! Certain Crystal's that end in -ite should not be placed in water. For example, Selenite will melt in water.)

If you don't prefer water, you can place it in a bowl of salt overnight. Allow the salt to extract any energetic attachments or negativity the pendulum may have picked up from hand to hand on its way to you. No magic words needed but a soft prayer of thanks will do.

If water or salt doesn't call to you, then we have sage! Sage is an ancient remedy for cleansing space and objects. Hold the pendulum in your hand and gently waft the sage smoke around the pendulum. I usually do a counterclockwise circle 9 times. Yes - I'm OCD but the number 9 is the number of completion in numerology. So 9 feels right to me. You can do 3 or 52, follow your instincts and let the pendulum tell you when it's cleansed.

Lastly, if water, salt, or sage is not an option. The Full Moon is your best bet! Place the stone outside on the night of a

Full Moon. The moon's light will cleanse, bless and charge your pendulum. I recommend doing one of the above options (water, salt or sage) plus the Full Moon. There is something magical about the Full Moon.

I place all my tools of magick outside during the Full Moon. Crystal's. Singing bowls. Divination tools. And projects I'm working on or crafts. Collect early in the morning as the sun is rising and you're golden! (If you sleep til noon - don't fret. Just watch the sunlight with Amethyst or Rose Quartz, these stones can fade in direct sunlight. Also - dew can be a problem for some stones and crafts.)

Alright - now we have cleansed the pendulum. Next comes what I like to call "programming." In some traditions, they call this step 'blessing and consecrating.' It's the same thing different name. Whether you call a cart, a shopping cart or a buggy, it still carries your groceries through the store.

Take the pendulum in your right hand, close your eyes and focus on your breath. As you relax, move your awareness to the pendulum in your hand. Feel its grooves along the inside of your palm. Is it warm or is it cool? Just notice. Just be. As you connect to your pendulum, tell it your intent.

"Please connect to Spirit in a way that is right and well for my highest good."

Part 2:

After you have blessed and programmed your pendulum. You can use it immediately!

For some, 'seeing' and 'journeying' to their guides is a bit tricky. (We will talk about that in the next lesson.) A tried and true method of divining information from your Spirit Guides is the use of a pendulum.

When using the pendulum, it is best if you start out asking 'Yes' or 'No' questions. The reasoning for this is to discover how your pendulum will communicate to you. The pendulum will move in specific ways for specific answers.

For me, a 'Yes' response from my pendulum is a back and forth movement. I always envision the pendulum nodding 'yes' with this response.

Ask some questions that you know the answer will be 'yes.' And discover how your pendulum says 'yes.'

For example:

"Is the sky blue?"
"Is my name [insert your name]?"
Etc.

Now, ask your pendulum questions that you know are false or will receive a 'no' response to.

When my pendulum says, 'no', it moves from side to side. Similar to a person shaking their head 'no.'

For example:

"Is the sky auburn?"

"Is my name Medusa?"

"Is the Earth flat?"

Etc.

Your pendulum is similar to a Magic 8 ball. There is also the 'Maybe', 'Clarify', and 'Ask Later' responses. These are harder to divine with simple questions. My pendulum swings around in a circle for these responses. I always giggle when this happens, it reminds me of the 'Loading' screen with its spinning circle. Buffering in Spirit and waiting for connection. Trust me - it's just as frustrating.

Try to divine some answers that you DON'T know the answers to. Ask the pendulum to help you discover answers you've been dying to know!

For example:
"Will I get married?"
"Will I win the lottery"
"Does my Soul Mates name start with an 'A'?"
Etc.

The world is your oyster. Record the responses. Some may get a maybe. But some will get a definitive 'Yes' or 'No.' Just a word of caution, don't constantly ask the same question. Spirit is very patient but every being has their limits.

Part 3:

After you have practiced and familiarized yourself with your pendulums responses, it is now time to tap into your guides. You have been doing this all along! But if you are exceptionally sensitive, you may have been picking up answers from any number of sources. The pendulum is like a radio antenna, it picks up whatever you tune into. For the earlier exercises, you were tuning into your higher self. That is perfect to start out! But you probably innately knew the answers in your subconscious mind.

Call upon your power animal, and asked them to speak to your pendulum. Asked them questions about your life, about your path, and about your life purpose that they would only hold the answers to. Your power animal will become almost like your best friend in the spirit world. An ally to work with you and help you infuse your life with magic and power. Always used to cern ment when speaking with your power animal, sometimes they like to speak in mysterious ways and use riddles so that you have to think through the problems they don't just give it to you freely.

You are well on your way on the path of Enlightenment. Don't give up! Continue on this journey with me as we go into the next chapter and will explore more in depth and exciting adventures on this journey.

Chapter 5
The Hierophant

Power and wisdom he has gathered, The
spiritual esthetic is all that's mattered
Seekers come and bow before you, waking
dreams and portans for you.
Everlasting peace and grace,
Be wear the mask of pride on your face.

Eternal life for one and all, Listen gently for
spirits call
Element Earth
Zodiac Taurus
Blessing Understanding

Challenge Pride
"Religions happen when people don't get
the point of the message and blindly
worship the message and the messenger,
instead of grasping the gnosis inherent
within the words that the message
conveys."
~Nicholas de Vere

188

After taking several steps along the path, possibly becoming initiated or granted certification, we fall into the mindset that we are complete. We are done and there is no need to go further than we are right now. The Christian Priesthood is a good example. Ordained and sanctified in the mysteries, they stop growth, accept the dogma of their prescribed faith and stay in this level of understanding for the remainder of their lives.

The oasis of dogma is quite tempting. You have glimpsed heaven and everlasting. You have learned how to clear away many blocks and emotional problems but you are only half way along the path. Yes - the journey is tiring. Yes - you can stop here and remain here. The element related to this step is Earth. It is well and good to rest a bit here. But don't give into the fantasy that your journey is over. You have learned all you can about spirituality and faith. No - that is the greatest pitfall. Pride in faith. Pride in belief.

Many stop along this respite and chose to make a permanent home. That is the wrong way to approach this path. The lesson of Taurus is to continually keep moving. Resting is fine. Expression Li when you are weary and tired and you have learned a lot and you need time to meditate on the information and knowledge that you have gathered.

Mini experience awakening and then think they are finished that the cycle is done and the wheel is over. But all of life is continually moving forward. As CS Lewis said "further up and further in." Spirit is made of duality, opposite's, multiverses, grand designs and schemes that the human logic, the earthly logic, can't comprehend or understand. Part of this path is realizing that far is near, dark is light, and depths are high to spirit.

Beware of the folly of pride and thinking that your way is the only way. My way is not the only way. There is more than one path that leads to this peak of the sacred mountain. In Aquarius energy, we have to remember that intuition and one's personal path and sovereignty is the most important aspect to this journey. Spirit is constantly communicating to you and letting you know the further steps that you need to take to move forward. Don't be stubborn like the bull and think that just because you have taken several steps that you are truly finished, that could not be further from the truth.

It is at this step that many believe they have what I like to call a false awakening. Where they have finished steps 1 through 4 but they haven't finished to the end and started the cycle over rebirth regeneration renewal.

It is at this time, that you stop and reflect on where you have come from and look forward to where you are going. Take this time to take your worries and cares to spirit. Instead of becoming the Hierophant become the Supplicant. Don't fall into the delusion that you have all the answers. Fall into the real reality that you are but a journeyer along the path. Spirit is constantly guiding you forward

Stand tall in growth that you've made. Rejoice in changes that have been wrought in your life. But fall to your knees in an overwhelming understanding and conviction that you are but human and you are moving towards ascension.

That is the greatest lesson in this chapter.

Lesson 9:

Finding Your World Tree

In a healing tarot deck that I use in my practice, the Hierophant is portrayed by a tree-like humanoid.

His steadfastness is grounding and his message is center to the Earth. Breathe deeply in the air and sunlight to stand and watch a visitor apart from the crowd.

The World Tree is sacred and magical to many cultures. Norse mythology especially hailed Yggdrasil as the center of the cosmos, birthplace of all life and bridge between worlds. The byfrost ringed the world tree like bypasses over valleys and mountains guiding travelers to others places to other world entirely. The Eagle perched at the top and a Snake slithered around the roots, a Squirrel tattered back and forth between the two exchanging insults and information. The world tree is one of the amazing As Above, So Below aspects of our world.

Think about your brain as the top of the world tree, able to conceive and create grand concepts and paradigms. Your feet are the roots, giving you foundation and constantly taking in information from the world around you. The spine is like the squirrel running information back and forth between the two spheres. Our mind and our body are not the same entities. Your body can have "a mind of its own." Your brain can be abusive and talk you down. As we learned in the Silent Witness exercise, you are both and you are more. You are and you aren't - one of the most transcendental dichotomies to grasp and reconcile on our path of Enlightenment. When you realize that you are so much more than your mind you break free of the chains of Ego and begin to explore the surrounding areas of your consciousness that help unlock the gates of ascension.

For this exercise, I want you to find a tree that you feel a connection with. The tree can be in your yard, in a favorite park, or on a picturesque trail or even hidden in an ancient grove that whispers of ancient times passed. Find a tree that speaks to you. You may already have one in mind. If you do, great! You're a step ahead of many of us. For the rest of us, search your surrounding area. Visit parks and walk some trails. Get out and explore Mother Nature.

Hiking became an important part of my journey. When I was with a past partner, we would go hiking all the time. We would walk in companionable silence and enjoy the views. Every now and then we would talk about stuff but mostly the hike was meditative. Feel each foot fall. Find your center. Adjust your posture as you were walking. Take each step with precision and you lessen the risk of injury when you are vigilant and present in your body. I look back on those memories with fondness and love for all things. I felt so connected!

One of these hikes, we hiked the Crystal Bridges trail in Bentonville, AR. Lined with art and sculptures that blend perfectly into the serene landscape of the Ozarks, I found a tree that was my World Tree. The tree is a cedar. It's gnarled and has limbs that stretch in every direction conceivable from its thick trunk. Some roots are exposed and they twist and turn in mind bending angles. I love that tree. When we walked by I instantly noticed it. I felt power thrumming through its limbs and the trunk felt warm to my touch. We stopped for a minute to rest and I placed my hand on the trunk. I felt a zap of electricity and then a little branch fell high from the top of the tree. It landed between my partner and I. We both looked at each other wide eyed. I picked it up and put the branch in my pack. I still have that branch and use it to connect to my tree when I need a recharge.

Cedars are ancient symbols of power and healing. Cedar can be used to smudge a room and cleanse illness from the body and spirit. Cedar is sacred in Celtic mythology, Christianity and to many Native tribes in North America. I'm happy my tree was a cedar. After our meeting, I noticed that cedar had always been in my life. Each residence I have ever lived at has a cedar tree. A silent sentinel that guards and protects the land. Wise and prosperous trees.

Find your tree. Commune with the spirit of the tree. Feel the energy pulsing around you.

Take a few moments to sit near or on your tree. I like to sit and lean back. My back and head connecting to the trunk. I like to look up and watch the wind and sunlight dance through the branches. Breathe deeply through your nose and inhale the earthy scent of the surrounding air. Trees are magical.

When you're ready, create a Merkabah and close your eyes while touching your tree.

Visit the world tree and ask that the world tree show you more about your tree. Commune with the world tree as you are communing with your tree. Touch its bark. Sit and lean against its solid trunk.

Look up, take in whatever sights are there. Breathe deeply. Feel the energy of Tree Spirit fill you with strength, fortitude and warmth.

Thank both trees and return to normal awareness. Drink some water to shake off the fuzzy feeling after a journey. The experience you had is a very transformative one.

The tree may gift you a branch or a leaf or some token of sorts. Wait and see what happens. You may take one. But ask your tree before taking anything. Pour out some water near the roots in thanks.

Once a connection is established. You can journey to your tree anytime you need a pick me up. Or information about herbs and Earth energies. Or for protection and strength. You are creating a partnership. A symbiotic relationship that helps connect you deeper with Gaia.

We are all her children. As such we must respect our environment and be the caretakers of this edenic world we inhabit.

We bless her - She blesses us in return.

What you get - give. We have lost that simple rule of life somewhere along the way. Fear makes us hold onto our love, our hopes, our possessions. Love acts us to set them free. Give freely! Remember - we are all freely given life. The present moment is a gift. Use your time wisely and share in gratitude with one another.

What a beautiful world we live in!

Lesson 10:

A Holy Sacrament

Every religion has ritual and ceremony. Many of the adherents and faithful don't understand the holy rites that they take part in. The ceremony is a hollow one. One of habit rather than conviction.

A ritual is a promise. A ceremony of intent marking growth, conviction and transformation from an old way of being or old beliefs and stepping into a new creation. Your being is transformed in a heartfelt, personal ritual.

During this exercise, we will be saying goodbye to the person we were and being born anew to who we are becoming. Similar to a baptism or an initiation, you will shed who you once were and step into a new life!

Supplies:

A cup filled with your favorite drink

A piece of bread or cake or a cookie

A gift for Spirit (herbs, flowers, money or
something personal to you)

Search "Dhyaanguru" on YouTube, play the
video titled "*Warning* Secret Monk Sounds
for Brain Activation and Healing

Ready your space by collecting all the items
you will need. Hold a meditative and
respectful attitude. We will be calling Deity
into our circle. Respect is necessary.
Ancestors and guides will walk with you.

Give gratitude from the start as you feel the energy beginning to build.

Place all your supplies in the center of your chosen space.

Begin to play the video. Allow the Theta waves to wash through your space as you continue to set up.

Create Sacred space like we learned in lesson One.

Stand in the center of your circle.

Raise your arms in a V shape and evoke Deity. Palms facing upward.
(As Above)

"Holy Father, Holy Mother! I, [insert your name], petition you now!"

Lower your arms in an upside down V.
Palms facing downward.
(So Below)

"Welcome to the circle. I have called you here to bare witness to my transformation. To celebrate my milestone. To release the self of the past and carry forward into the Light!
Shine upon me and raise me up that I might be a Light for the world."

Sip from your cup. Place the rest aside for later.

Take a bite of the bread. Place the rest
aside for later.

Hold the gift next to your heart.

And say,

"The gift I hold was dearly sought and dearly
    wrought. I give to you a small token of my
    thanks. May my token be accepted as you
    have accepted and loved me. An exchange
        of gifts for each of us!"

Stand for a moment. Continue to hold the
gift in your hands. Deity may speak to you at
this time. Open your eye, open your mind,
open your heart to receive.

Gifts will be given to you. Or awakened in you as you open to Spirit. Spirit has so much to show you. Let it all soak in. Let the Light pour into you.

Place the gift near the drink and the bread.

Place your hands across your chest, crossed in a warm hug.

"Thank you for the gifts that you always bestow upon me! The gifts of life, love, lessons and journeys! My heart is full and I am whole again."

Thank Deity for attending your ceremony in a way that suits you.

Sit in reflection for the remainder of the song. Create the Merkabah and allow Spirit to continue to guide your ritual in this time and in this space. You may go to different worlds. You may be invited to the throne room itself. You may walk lush hills or down into deep forests. Follow the pull and go where you feel drawn.

When the song comes to a close, pull back your awareness to the present.
Take another sip of the drink and nibble a piece of the bread.

Take the rest and pour out your drink and place the bread outside near a tree or flower bed, if you are able.

Place the gift in a place that is sacred to you. The tree found in our last lesson would do nicely.

Meditate and journal on your experience. Jot down insights. Any gifts you received. And look for those gifts to arrive in the physical. They will appear as if by magic, especially if it was a gem, or a feather or a plant. You will find the gift in the physical world.

Bless you Seeker! You are half way there.

Tonight, let go of the cares of the world and celebrate!!! Celebrate your new life! Celebrate the new you!!!

You're so worth it!!!

Chapter 6
The Lovers

Choosing knowledge and paradise lost,

Waking from slumber night has tossed

The Angel sounds the mighty trump,

Judgement day has broken tree to a stump.

An apple for wisdom stands,

Distraction is the con of man.

Element: Air

Zodiac: Gemini

Blessing: Union

Challenge: Distraction

Adam and Eve were the primordial man and woman. Tossed out of the garden of Eden for eating the Tree of the Knowledge of Good and Evil. God told them they would die if they ate of the tree. And so they did.

Fallen from heaven, they were plunged into a body of flesh and blood - forgetting all memory of the higher dimensions they were just walking in. The fall affected us all. Humanity fell from the higher dimensions into the realm of the 3d world. As each soul is born, it forgets its true nature. Our true purpose is hidden by the dreams and hopes that society, peer pressure and parental figures place on our tiny minds. We know innately there is something more. We seek that other out. There is a certain *je ne sais quoi* that we all try to find but seem to forget over and over.

That is evidence of the fall. The Fool's Journey is about finding that hidden identity. Like peeling back layers of the onion, we reconnect with our Divine Masculine and Divine Feminine. We eat once again of the Tree of Life. The fruit provides us with the long sought after elixir of life. We experience soul alchemy. Our souls are transmuted into the driving force that governs our lives. When the union of Divine Feminine/Masculine takes place, a shift occurs in the individual. Balance is paramount. Unity of duality is ascension.

If you are like me, you know you can't over eat or you'll gain weight. You can't over exercise or you'll injure yourself. Yet lack of exercise leaves your body aching and working harder to keep equilibrium. Breathing gets hard. Steps that were once a piece of cake become Mt. Everest. Too much sex and you're letting other parts of your life slide. Not enough sex and you become aggressive or moody. Life is all about maintaining balance. Light and dark. They all dwell within us. Spirit designed that duality so that we might experience 'free will.' The choice between good and evil. Pleasure or pain. Light or dark. In the 3d realm that is the parameters of this reality.

When we begin to ascend, that duality blends. You are no longer good or bad. You are neither and you are both. You are both out and both in. As you journey on this path you may seem to fade in and out of reality. That is okay! You're traveling higher roads. Your vibration is rising. Your power is humming in your veins. You are living a life with one foot in and one foot out. People may say you're not the same. You're not fully present. And of course - they are right.

I'm not going to lie. Think about oil and water. They separate when placed in a cup and left undisturbed. You can mix and blend with the 3d realm but eventually you split and separate. Friends, family, lovers, jobs and others will begin to break away. This is natural. This is for your highest good. You are simply not in harmony with them anymore. To stay there will cause disharmony and dissonance. The disharmony will manifest as fights, arguments, pain and suffering if you try to stay in their vibe. When people walk away from you, they are not for you.

Learning to discern your tribe by their vibe is important. You will unconsciously gravitate towards people with similar beliefs, vibes and frequencies as you. Like calls to like. Do not be afraid of this process. You will feel the pull. Go with it. Struggling will only make this step 10xs harder. I assure you.

I struggled for 12 years. I wanted to stay in my relationship. I was growing and growing, exponentially in spirit and heart. I was literally dragging my partner with me. His body suffered, my body suffered. Our relationship became tumultuous as we no longer spoke each other's language. I was running, they were walking. That pace won't last for long, inevitably you trip over one another and take a fall.

Then you are left swimming from the wreckage and trying to grab at any debris to keep you afloat. Luckily, the steps and lessons from earlier help deal with this. For a time you may be alone. That is okay. You need time to heal, grow and become. Every seed must cleave from the flower and its friends and take to the ground alone. Shoved into the dark, under intense pressure and solitude it grows into its own flower!

The step of the lovers is similar. Follow your intuition.

Be open to the universe turning your life upside down. What Spirit takes away, it replaces. When you are purging emotions and memories, you are making room for the new and better future! Don't be afraid to expand and grow. When the flower is not growing well, you don't fix the flower - you fix the environment. You change the pot. Change the soil.

Life is much the same. Growing means you may outgrow your current circumstances. Your hometown may become too small. Or you may get fed up with your 9 to 5 and start your own business! That is the goal of this journey! Find your calling and present the best version of yourself to others and thus to the world.

"Raise the Vibe! Heal the Tribe!"
Bradley Philpott

In the next two lessons, we will visit both aspects of Godself or Deity. The Divine Masculine and the Divine Feminine. Be sure to practice both exercises. Whether you are Christian, Wiccan, agnostic or other, balance in Deity and in life is key. Balance will help you understand all of humanity better. By knowing all aspects of yourself, you will be empowered to heal those aspects in others by living your truth and walking in balance.

Lesson 11:

Journey to The Divine Masculine

Supplies:

Ceremonial Tools

Offering to The Divine Masculine

Set up your space in a meditative manner. We will be journeying to the archetypal Divine Masculine. Use any items or pieces that relate to the male aspect of Godself. You may want to visit YHWH, God of the Jewish Tradition. Zeus may be more up your alley. Apollo, Odin, Cerenunus, The Green Man, Father Sky are all possible options for this exercise.

Create Ritual space as prescribed in Lesson 1.

Stand in the center of your circle. Raise your arms in V shape. Lift your head to the sky and speak with conviction.

"All Father! Holly Man! Mighty Warrior of man! Conqueror of worlds! Gentle teacher!

223

Keeper of mysteries of life, death and rebirth! Come and sit with me. Let us commune together!"

Now lay down and go into a state of relaxation. Create the Merkabah around you for protection of body and spirit.

Follow the 12 step countdown to visit the world tree.

When you approach the world tree, there will be a bench or seat to sit on. Sit and call to the Divine Masculine as you see this aspect of Deity. Wait until he arrives.

When he arrives, respectfully ask that your masculine aspect of self be healed.

If you are prompted by deity, ask any burning questions. About life, your soul path and your true purpose.

Offer your offering. When back in the physical realm, leave the offering at your World Tree in the 3d plane.

Deity may speak with you for a while. Absorb any messages or gifts that are given to you. Feel the Divine Masculine within yourself be healed and awakened. Balance in all aspects of life are important.

After you are through, thank Godself for visiting with you.

Depart the way you came. Return to your physical body, release the circle, drink some water and nibble on a snack to get back into your body.

Sit for a while and meditate on what you have learned. Jot down insights and messages in your journal.

How do you feel?
What aspects of the Divine Masculine were healed through this visit?
Ponder the messages you received.

Lesson 12:

Journey to The Divine Feminine

Supplies:

Ceremonial Tools

Offering to The Divine Feminine

Set up your space in a meditative manner. We will be journeying to the archetypal Divine Feminine. Use any items or pieces that relate to the female aspect of Godself. You may want to visit Sophia, Goddess of Wisdom from the Jewish tradition. Isis, Hera, Diana of the Moon, The Triple Goddess, Hecate, Brigid, or Freyja are all aspects of the Goddess that resonate with the archetypal Feminine.

Create Ritual space as prescribed in Lesson 1.

Stand in the center of your circle. Raise your arms in V shape. Lift your head to the sky and speak with conviction.

"Holy Mother! Fertile Lush Earth Goddess! Vengeful Protector of man! Steward of the Garden! Gracious teacher! Bearer of mysteries of life, death and rebirth! Come and sit with me. Let us commune together!"

Now lay down and go into a state of relaxation. Create the Merkabah around you for protection of body and spirit.

Follow the 12 step countdown to visit the world tree.

When you approach the world tree, there will be a bench or seat to sit on. Sit and call to the Divine Feminine as you see this aspect of Deity. Wait until he arrives.

When she arrives, respectfully ask that the feminine aspect of self be healed.

If you are prompted by deity, ask any burning questions. Ask about life, your soul path and your true purpose.

Offer your offering. When back in the physical realm, leave the offering at your World Tree in the 3d plane.

Deity may speak with you for a while. Absorb any messages or gifts that are given to you. Feel the Divine Feminine within yourself be healed and awakened. Balance in all aspects of life are important.

After you are through, thank Godself for visiting with you.

Depart the way you came. Return to your physical body, release the circle, drink some water and nibble on a snack to get back into your body.

Sit for a while and meditate on what you have learned. Jot down insights and messages in your journal.

How do you feel?
What aspects of the Divine Feminine were healed through this visit?
Ponder the messages you received.

Chapter 7
The Chariot

Thundering hooves over glassy water,

Time stops and can't be bothered.

The sun races across the sky,

The moon follows softly she glides.

To run the race is the biggest sham,

Steady onward is the task at hand.

Element: Water

Zodiac: Cancer

Blessing: Control

Challenge: Chaos

Wow! What an experience of balance and integrating the whole of who you are into self. The last two lessons are important and vital exercises to practice often. As we move in and out of 3d reality, our pendulum of balance is thrown off balance. The Chariot reminds us that the work is always happening. Time is steadily marching forward. We may be able to move in and out of different timelines. We can visit past and future with simply a thought.

That is the secret and mystery of the Sphinx. Two sphinxes lead the Chariot onward. They walk through time and space. The work is never done. Rest is essential as we learned in Chapter Five. In this Chapter, we will talk about the importance of temperance and perseverance. The work we strive towards is a life of balance.

Many cultures speak of this sacred work. The Tao calls this union Tao. Christianity calls this marriage Sanctity. For me, I call this mystery Ascension. Finding balance within oneself is essential to living a happy and prosperous life. We often seek completion in others. We think that we can find wholeness outside of ourselves. That is simply not true.

Marriage itself sprang from this desire to create union within each of us. But the real gnosis is understanding that wholeness comes from within and pours outward. To be complete inside is to be able to be completely loving and understanding of all life. Only then are you truly ready for the path of marriage.

Cancer rules this step. Cancer is all about emotions. Emotions are generally tied to water. Like water, emotions come and go. They flow undeterred by logic or expression. Learning to harness their power versus being controlled by them is key. We balanced the Sacred Yin and Yang within our spirits in the last chapter. Now - let's talk about emotions. It is time to conquer that steady stream.

Emotions are signals from the subconscious that something is either good or bad for the self. When we are in a toxic situation for our true self, we experience anger, fear and anxiety. When we are in healthy situations we experience bliss, happiness and love. Emotions are essential to living life in a healthy way.

Our modern society treats emotions in a very upside down way. We say, "I am sad" or "I am happy." Do you remember talking about "I am" statements earlier in our journey? How would saying "I am sad" throw off the balance of your entire self? As you guessed, that "I am" statement can throw us into a tailspin of depression and anxiety. Our soul can be crushed under that mental projection. The Universe hears "I am sadness" and all your life moves to resonate within that vibration. Our world becomes dark and dreary as we continue to project that "sadness."

Saying those statements sends out a signal, we must be conscious of what we are projecting out into the world. Our reality is our own creation. We are co-creators of this world.

On the other hand, "I am happy" has a positive affect on our reality. Try saying that phrase even when you are not. Watch as your spell ripples out and returns happiness to you. Being the ruler of your emotions does not mean you stop feeling stress, anxiety or pain. No - instead you use those emotions as simply alarms that something in your life is not serving your highest good. And then project "I am loved," "I am happy," or "I am whole." Be the steward of your emotions, not their prisoner. Learn to manifest exactly what you need versus what you're experiencing. The greatest joy can be found in hardship and the greatest contentment can be found in every situation. If only you would choose it.

LESSON 13:
Stewards of Our Garden

Our emotions are only alert systems in our body. Helping us navigate the waters of life. Life is filled with ups and downs but we can stay the course and create a sense of stability and balance within the chaos. We cannot control the outside world, but the internal world within us is our domain to create and rule.

During my study at John Brown University, I studied music and sound. Music is intrinsically healing. I call music the language or the soul. Music affects our physical body, our emotional body and our spirit deep within us. Like ripples in water, sound waves generate a reaction within our inner world. I warn my clients that music, art and entertainments are aspects of your diet. Food is essential for the physical body as fuel. Music and other sounds affect us in much the same way.

Have you ever listened to a song and your mood is lifted? Do you listen to a song and suddenly you're thrown into a past memory, one of joy or even heartbreaking pain? Music is powerful! Science is just beginning to understand how much sound waves affect our bodies. We already know music affects the mind. But what if I told you, music affects all aspects of your self? The body, mind and the spirit is affected by those squiggly waves of air. The waves pass through us and shift your vibration. For good or for ill.

In the chart below, you can see how different frequencies affect your mental and physical state. *

Delta patterns: Binaural beats in the delta pattern are set at a frequency of between 0.1 and 4 Hz, which is associated with dreamless sleep.

Theta patterns: Binaural beats in the theta pattern are set at a frequency of between 4 and 8 Hz, which is associated with sleep in the rapid eye movement or REM phase, meditation, and creativity.

Alpha pattern: Binaural beats in the alpha pattern are set at a frequency of between 8 and 13 Hz, which may encourage relaxation.

Beta pattern: Binaural beats in the beta pattern are set at a frequency of between 14 Hz and 100 Hz, which may help promote concentration and alertness. However, this frequency can also increase anxiety at the higher end of the frequency range.

Practice listening to some examples. Search the web for some Theta beats. These beats are best experienced with headphones.
Let's get our jam on! Find the rhythm in the beat!

Supplies:
Headphones
A video or music player
Theta beats track

Sit in your quiet place. Either in your room, a meditation room or near your World Tree.

When you are ready, begin the Theta Beats track.

You may create Sacred Space if you feel led, but it is not necessary for this exercise.

Start by relaxing your mind. Release the events and emotions of the day. Slowly move your awareness to your heart center.

Create the Merkabah. Open to the world around you. Simply be.

Tune in to the frequency of the Theta Beats. Allow the beats to raise your vibration and with it your mood and attitude.

Let emotions float by like leaves floating on a river.

Start an Affirmation and repeat the affirmation in your head with the beat. Keep the affirmation steady and rhythmic like a drum.

"I am loved.

I am worthy.

I am forgiven."

Allow the Theta Beats to reinforce your affirmation. Continue the affirmations and see how they ripple outward with the beats. As they go outward, the waves return inward just like a ripple in a pond.

Repeat this exercise as often as you need. Play around with different beats and different affirmations until you find a combination that clicks. You will feel when you succeed. The experience will be transcendent. The beautiful part is this is easily recreated over and over with any situation.

Use this to manifest money and abundance. Use this to manifest love and happiness. Use this to defeat depression and anxiety.

The power is yours!

*Chart of   beats
created   by Justin
Webb - a Seiðr shaman and friend of mine.

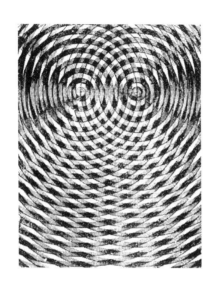

Lesson 14:

Ecstatic Beat

Supplies:

A drum or rattle

Or

Recording of shamanic drum beat

(120 bpm recommended)

Shamans of old practiced a different meditative experience than is usually taught in classes and workshops today. The experience was ecstatic! The meditation was visceral.

 Movement. Blood pumping. Exhilaration! As above, so below rings true here. You can reach the peak in quiet meditation, a steady walk. Or you can run up the peak, a hike that's invigorating and earth shaking.

We've used the gentle way up to this point. Now let's turn it up a notch.

Turn on the music or begin to beat your drum. Feel the rhythm. Move your hips. Dance to the beat. It doesn't matter what you look like, let the music take you.

Create sacred space as you learned in Lesson 1. As you do move and embody each element. Jump up and down with fire. Move sinuously and languid with air. Be supple and lithe with water. And stomp your feet with earth. Get into it. Your breath should be coming a little harder after all speaking and dancing.

Now, invite the God and the Goddess to the
Spiral dance!

Start in the East and begin a simple dance.
Step. Step. Spin. As you move slowly spiral
towards the center. Take your time. Feel

Spirit quicken within you. Feel the ancestors drums calling you inward.

It may take you a few moments or a while to reach the center. When you do. Lay down in the center. Feel your blood rushing. Your body thrumming with the beat. Close your eyes and just be.

You may experience visions or trance. Go with the experience. Let Spirit guide you. If you like, go to the World Tree and dance around the tree. Keep dancing - keep moving.

Feel the dance sear the blood in your veins. Quicken your breath and harden your body. Let ecstasy explode from you. Pure joy of movement and experience.

Welcome to the gift of the present!

This moment right now is all that matters.
Let everything else fade away and
experience the dance of ancient peoples
and tribes. Experience the school of
ecstasy!

After you are through, thank Deity and
release the circle.

Record your experiences in your journal.
How was this experience different than quiet
meditation?
Is this something you liked or disliked?
(Let me tell you a secret. If you disliked it,
good! Then you need to practice it more!
There is a block in your body that can only

253

be released when you let go and free your

body to move and experience.)

How do you feel right after?

Thank you for journeying with me!

Now we journey deeper.

Down into   Shadow.

The beast of old.

Chapter 8

Strength

The beast within growls and wakes.

The shadows creep and hide its face.

A gentle hand comes to close the maw.

Of agony, pain and sorrows wrought.

Compassion is the loving key.

Joy for all and glad tidings be.

Element: Fire

Zodiac: Leo

Blessing: Courage

Challenge: Fear

"Man has no enemy equal to the unenlightened mind. It is this unenlightened mind that has built up this vast structure of terrestrial selfishness, discord and greed. The false light or lower mind is the emblem of the beast and the number 666. The beast, consequently, is the uninspired mind which is opposed to the inspired or Divine Mind. This monster of the lower mind, this leviathan that swallows Jonah, this creature that comes out of the sea of illusion, this beast with the crown on his head —- all this symbolism refers to the unenlightened human intellect."

~ Manly P Hall

The Shadow. The great beast of old. Hell on Earth. Fire and Damnation.
Bold and stark imagery is used to describe the darkness in man. Our souls are dualistic. We each carry Light and Dark within our souls. That was the fall and the grace, the experience of free will.

In tribal culture, the shamanic initiation is brutal and harrowing experience. You are about to walk that ancient, trodden path. The time had come to meet your shadow.

The shadow aspect of our being is all the repressed fears, neglected desires and old wounds that we hide from ourselves. The shadow manifest as mental illness plagued by worry and anxiety, soul loss because that darkness has created a monster that we fear, and the quintessential demons that control and manipulate us during times of weakness. Demons are very real. And we each carry our own demons and burdens into our lives.

We drag them from relationship to relationship. We carry them as a chip on our shoulder. They are our innate fears, the primal urges that drive us to procreate and chase after money and power. We believe that we are inherently weak or inherently bad. But we are not. We are both strength and weakness. Good and bad resides within us all.

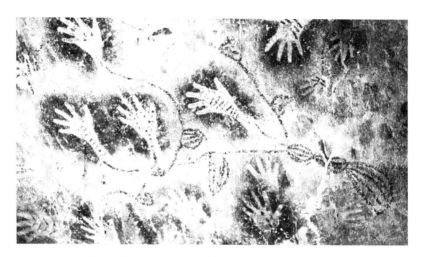

A 'panel' of hand stencils is pictured in the El Castillo Cave in Spain.

Shamans of old journeyed into ancient caves to face the shadow. They walked a marked path and used substances to induce a vision of their darker selves. This demon

258

or shadow would kill the shaman. He would be reborn after a journey into his darkest hell. Forever changed and healed from the wounds of his deep soul. He became shaman in truth, one who sees in the darkness. He sees his own darkness and succumbs to it, he doesn't fight it. He doesn't destroy it. He integrates it as an integral part of the whole. We are all shadows and light.

Mine happened very much like the shaman's journey. Except mine took years. I carried darkness around and spewed hate at everyone and anything that thought they loved me. Convinced I was the demon. You see we either give in to the Light of ourselves and want to be holy, pure and good. Or we choose anger, darkness and wrath. I thought I was unlovable because I bought into the lie that I was evil and bad person. I was my shadow. I fought the integration of the shadow. I fought against the true gift of the shadow. Balance. And learning compassion for others fighting their own inner demons.

In fact, many of us fight the shadow. We don't want to accept darkness. We are bearers of Light. We are the Light workers of the world! How can we have darkness?

And that is our greatest folly - pride. Pride that we are any better than another human being. We are no more and we are no less. We are all a blend of light and shadow.

A beautiful analogy I use is one of a white tower. We work on nothing but the Light. We grow in the light. We become a bulwark, a light house of Light. A place of healing for the weary and the weak. But what happens when the sun shines on a tall tower? The taller the tower - the longer the shadow it creates. The fear and bad aspects you see in others are but reflections of the shadow in yourself.

Continue forward to embrace your shadow and die to who you think you are. Be made new. A shaman. A sage. A witch. A healer. In truth, you are about to be whole. Your breakthrough is here.

The key is in your hand. Take it and unlock the door!

Lesson 15:

The Archer Shoots the Soul Wound

Supplies:

A drum or rattle

Or

Recorded shamanic drumming

Prepare your space in a meditative manner.

Cleanse and prepare yourself with a ritual cleansing. Take a luxurious bath or shower and scrub away the old. You are about to be reborn.

You won't need any supplies for this journey. All you need is a brave and compassionate heart. A willingness to grow. The seed of hope.

Begin to drum. Play your recorded track. Feel the music. Get into your body and feel the groove. Wiggle your special dance.

Create sacred space as described in lesson one.

Call Deity to the circle. Ask that the God and Goddess guide your path to your shadow self.

Perform the Spiral Dance as we learned in the last lesson. Follow the pattern inward. As you dance towards the center let your awareness draw inward to your heart center.

When you reach the center, collapse and lay down. Create the Merkabah. Protect your body and spirit with your power animal.

When you are ready, close your eyes and journey to the World Tree. With your power animal beside you, build a sacred fire from the limbs and brush around the tree. Light the fire with your mind.

Dance with your power animal around the fire. As you do, call to your shadow self to come and join the dance.

"Shadow of my soul. Come. Dance with me. Be free and let me see your true form!"

While you continue to dance, you notice a shape dancing across the fire from you. The shape will be dark. It may be a monster, a shadow or just you but with a darker edge. Do not fear.

You draw closer and closer to one another.

All of a sudden you are standing face to face with your shadow.

Raise your arms and embrace your shadow. Send it love. Send it compassion. Send the shadow acceptance.

Step back and ask the shadow to show you your soul wound that needs healing.

The shadow will draw a bow or knife.

Stand tall and raise your arms out to your sides palms up.

"I am ready. Aim true!"

The shadow will shoot you or make a strike towards you. The blow will hurt. It will send searing pain through your being.

Locate the wound. Watch as black blood flows out of you. A cleansing and a deep healing is taking place.

Let the blood flow. As it does, thank your shadow and bid it walk in love with you. It will fade away or fade into you.

As the blood flows, watch as it flows black to red and then to shining gold. When it is golden. Feel the warmth healing your every scar. Your every hurt. Your every trauma.

Close your hands over the wound and ask the God and the Goddess to help you heal and seal the wound. Light with emanate for a brief moment as you feel your flesh weave and knit back together.

Return to your body.

Thank deity and release the circle.

Jot down the experience in your journal.

Where was the wound?

What message did you receive?

Meditate and home the blessing of the

shadow close to your heart.

You are new! You are reborn!

Chapter 9

The Hermit

He has walked the path of Night,

Changed he be, a new creation with new sight.

His steps trodden the path of Light.

A fiery birth, a lush grove, caverns with crystals bright.

The staff in one hand he stands on faith.

The lantern held aloft to usher in the gate.

Make a wish and time will tell.

Fairy rings and forgotten spells.

Element: Earth

Zodiac: Virgo

Blessing: Wisdom

Challenge: Conceit

You have walked the path. The journey is almost at an end.

You have done the work. You have gained wisdom and knowledge. You have taken back your power. Small pieces will always remain. Power is like the tide in that power ebbs and flows following focus and intent. We are constantly diverting power or drawing it in.

There are some souls that would use this against you. From no fault of their own, whether they are weak, or have their power bled out constantly or they seek dominion over others, emotional and psychic vampires exist. Being a Light requires sacrifice, hard work and dedication. Others would take what you fought so valiantly for. They want the reward without the work. They want the product without having to pay.

For a long time, I attracted partners that needed healing. They came to me with issues, as we all have. Like a moth to a flame they were drawn to my light. They wanted my light but didn't want to do the work to make their own light shine. You see the Light comes from a combination of experiences and a mindset. I can teach someone until I'm blue in the face but until they are ready to make a change or to grow, there is only so much I can do. When they realize you can't help them, people get angry, resentful and combative. They want your shine but they don't want to truly dig deep enough to let their own light out.

The most important mindset of all is Choose Love. I have harped on this over and over throughout this book and I will hop on my soap box once more.

Love is the answer.

Love is all you need. Love is the frequency and most powerful magic in existence. Simple and yet so profound. I don't mean romantic love. But yes, that's a facet of real love. I mean unconditional, unchanging, everlasting love for everyone around you.

Love of self is essential to be healthy and ready when others call out to you for help.

You can't love others until you love yourself. Love pours outward.

Love of others and compassion for where they are along this journey. Maybe they aren't even to The Fool stage yet. Maybe they are still asleep. Show them the same compassion as a brother or sister of the light.

The sage loves all. Yet does not need another to sustain them. He does not need his base desires met. He realizes they are just that - basic. He shuns the traditional idea of hearth and home. He makes lodgings outside the generic parameters. Hermits and wise ones have always been found on the outskirts of society. As bridges to the other realms, their life mirrors that "half in - half out." As above, so below. Caves, groves, grottoes, cottages on the edge of the wild are where he feels at home. Close enough that they can get food and supplies when times are tough and that people can seek them out but not close enough to be immersed in the day to day drama that is modern human community.

When you walk the Path of Light, you do not have to forgo modern convenience and go live in a cave. Instead you have to trust in Spirit. You allow Spirit to choose your accommodations. You let unconditional love guide your relationships. You surrender your life to the divine. The ritual to do this is rather simple but powerful and effective.

The final gift I can give you is to return you to your full power.

I can show you how to return to full sovereignty over your life's journey. When you pull your power back, you do the world a great service. You let each person and thing exist on its own. You no longer have any attachments. You no restrict their nature. And you are free to be who you were truly meant to be.

As we journeyed from the Fool to the Hermit, you have changed. You have grown exponentially from day one and you will continue to grow as you progress down the path. You have taken back power and learned ways to alter your reality. You can now guide your mind and body to newer heights. Continue the exercises and continue taking back your power. Be the light by being a shining example of self love and love for others. Kindness begets kindness.

"Teach love by embodying love.
Teach devotion by embodying devotion.
Teach surrender by embodying surrender."
-Madalyn Elizabeth Love

Lesson 16:

Release the Ties That Bind

Supplies:

Theta Beats Music

Cleanse and prepare your body for ritual in a way that suits you. Take a nice bath. Enjoy a soak. Relax and unwind.

Prepare your space in a meditative and respectful state.

Turn on the Theta Music.

Create Sacred Space. Cleanse the area and call in Deity.

"Father & Mother! I come to you changed and renewed. I ask that you guide my path from this point forward. Thank you for loving me when I was unlovable. I want to return that love to all."

Lay down or sit in a comfortable position.

Follow the 12 step countdown and go into trance. You may use the ecstatic experience if you prefer.

Journey to the World Tree.

When you reach the base of the trunk, there will be a fire waiting. The God and the Goddess stand next to the flames.

They usher you forward.

"Who comes?" Calls a voice of many waters.

"[State Your Name]"

"Do you truly wish to love all mankind?"
Asks a multitude of ancestors. Their arms
linked in a circle around you.

"Yes!"

"Then come to the flames."
Says the God.

"Be reborn!"
Says the Goddess.

You are prompted to remove your clothes. You are born naked and so shall you be reborn.

As you walk towards the flame, you notice green strings attached to every part of your body. Each one is siphoning energy away from your heart, pulling power from your soul.
They singe in the fire.

At the moment of truth, you do not hesitate -

You enter the flames.

The flames sear the cords that bound you to the physical world. They rend each connection and you are truly set free. You feel so light you could fly.

282

And you do!!!

You soar and rise from the ashes, as Phoenix. A new creation. A babe again.

"Welcome to the tribe" you hear a chorus of loved one's say as you take to wing and fly wherever your wings may take you.

Be free!

Soar!

When you are through, thank Deity for walking you through this milestone.

Release the circle.

Drink and nibble some food while you take out your journal.

Record your experiences.

What did you experience?
How do you feel after your journey?
Where did you fly to?
Why did you make this journey?

Choose love!!!
Do not give in to fear.

The battle is almost won!

Chapter 10

Wheel of Fortune

Around and around and around the wheel goes.

When it will stop and the world fall away?

Nobody knows.

The time and place do not even matter.

The chaos and fates are mad as a hatter.

The lesson is this:

You begin again, day by day.

All life is a cycle, learn that - escape!

Element: Ether

Zodiac: N/A

Blessing: Rebirth

Challenge: Repeating Patterns

From the acolyte Fool to the wise Hermit and back again. All of life plays in a loop. You get to repeat lessons again and again. Don't worry if you failed, the universe will make sure you learn and grow. The powers that be will give you better wisdom, more power and more heart to combat the dragon a second time. You are in good hands. Your own!

Trust me - I have ridden the wheel over and over again. Each time I learned more and more. I got the answers right eventually. Be patient with yourself. Don't take your life too seriously. Magic is found when you let love and laughter rule instead of fear and anger.

Choose love above all things!
Release the fear and live in the gift of the present!

The New Earth is here and now. You don't have to wait for a rapture talked about in a book written 2,000 years ago. The ascension is occurring. The dead in Christ are rising and oh! the stories they have to tell. Your young men are having visions of the future. Your young women are dreaming dreams. Every thing is not as it seems. Prophecies and visions are winsome things. Interpretation takes intuition and higher guidance. I'm sure many pulpits have proclaimed this very fact. But in our society, the heart is where we lack. Discernment is key and portents will abound. The coming of a new age is around.

Rise up and walk into the portals and into the Light. Stay and be plunged into 3d and night. The harder you fight, the worse it will be. For every man shall fall on bended knee. Chances are given time and time again. Take up your walking stick and ascend!

Blessings!

Meet Bradley!

Visit my webpage to book services and for workshop information:

Visit me on Facebook:

www.facebook.com/wildfirenearth

The Human Experience:

www.facebook.com/TheHumanExperienceLLC

YouTube:

https://www.youtube.com/channel/
UCAkaffTwS-AYbamXo_B2pAw

Come on a journey with me!

Have you heard about ascension, the rapture, or transcendence? Are downloads coming in at all hours of the night or during your daily routine? Have you seen visions of a future that seem to come true? Are your dreams wispy and thin yet at other times vivid and wild with meaning? Has your world been turned upside down by loss, heartbreak, growth or expansion? Are you on the path of enlightenment?

You may be experiencing The Shift, you are a member of the Rainbow Tribe. Learn to be a beacon of Light in a world ruled by Darkness. Following the ancient journey of the Fool, from babe to wise sage, you will learn tools, techniques and magics to aide you along your path of enlightenment!

We are the Rainbow Tribe that many Native Americans prophesied of long ago. As you journey through these pages, you will learn ancient teachings and how to apply them with modern understanding. The world is shifting.
Are you ready to take up the torch and light the way?

You can learn to harness your power, fine tune your spiritual gifts and shine brightly to be an anchor of Light for this world. You will become like a lighthouse and shine for all to see. Your vibration will help raise the collective vibration of your community, your nation and ripple outward to heal the Earth.

"Raise the Vibe - Heal the Tribe!"
Bradley Scott, Reiki Master/Teacher, Hipster Shaman, Intuitive Psychic Medium
Jack of All Trades & Master of Nothing